'Do we need yet another
Andy's leadership acume
Read this and be inspired
from someone who is the
compassionate leadership, and sees the best in everyone
he meets! I found reading this book was an opportunity to
"Walk with the wise" and to learn some golden lessons in
what makes good leaders great.'
Chris Duffett, Co-Principal of The Light College and former President of the Baptist Union

'Releasing and inspiring the emerging generations is one of
our greatest opportunities and biggest challenges as a
church. The pages of the Bible and Church history are full of
young people doing extraordinary things for God. *The Now
Generation* captures the urgency, wisdom and inspiration
required to unleash not the Church of tomorrow, but the
Church of today. Andy Monks has crafted a significant work
crammed full of quality advice, engaging stories and hard-
hitting quotes. I'm excited for the Now Generation – may
they read this book and live it!'
Phil Knox, Evangelical Alliance and author of Story Bearer

'Andy Monks is a young talent to watch. He brings humble
but distilled wisdom to what it means to lead, and this flows
from his own experience and insight into God's heart and
character.'
Glyn Jones, Co-Principal of the Light College

'In *The Now Generation*, Andy Monks has created an
accessible and rich resource for young people in particular to
reach their full potential. By using his own experience and
lessons learned, along with memorable analogies and

summaries, Andy provides a tool to equip those who are stepping into leadership. This will be such a helpful and valuable book for many.'
Carolyn Skinner, CEO Third Space Ministries

'This book is all the things I wish I could have read instead of finding them out the hard way – alone! After reading, you come away feeling empowered. Andy Monks, myself and Whitney Houston share the same belief that children are our future and we must allow them to lead. Not only are YOU the future, but the future is YOURS. So read this book that is full of wisdom – go out and lead your way!'
Kathryn Lord, award-winning author and child education expert; founder of More to Books and More to Organising

'*The Now Generation* is a rallying call to all young people to step into their God-given identity as influencers for good and for God. It is a manifesto of encouragement, inspiration and perspiration and will be a great tool for young people as they look to embrace all that God has for them right here, right now.'
Marcus Gibbs, Vicar, Ascension Balham

'It is sometimes said that "leadership is influence". In his insightful and practical book, Andy Monks expounds this maxim magnificently. He illustrates that growth in our leadership is not to be found in acquisition of status or position, but in increasing our sphere and potency of influence. This relational concept of leadership is not just biblically compelling but also resonates deeply with the generation of now and the emerging millennial generation. Andy's book will inspire and equip many, and he sets out his case in a way that is eminently readable, persuasive and empowering.'

Greg Downes, Kingfisher Ministries and former Dean of the Wesley Centre at Wycliffe Hall, Oxford University

'I was expecting *The Now Generation* to excite me about the influence young people can have in God's kingdom and in leadership, but it has met and exceeded all my expectations! I found myself hooked on every golden nugget of advice, Andy's vulnerable and inspiring story illustrations, and the positive and practical application points that he shares throughout this book. It has not only ignited in me a new passion for young leaders and raised my expectancy of how capable young people are of great influence; but it has personally brought me freedom and clarity in my own leadership journey.

'Andy has a gift of communicating powerful processes in such a simple and accessible way. This book is a must-read for all who are looking to grow in positively influencing those around them. Andy's teachings humble and reassure us of our own human limitations while bringing hope by always pointing back to the power and firm foundation we have in Jesus. This book transcends the age of the reader, yet especially enables, equips and empowers young leaders to step into their God-given power and calling. I am excited by how God will use Andy's words to raise, shape and guide people to be positive leaders in this "Now Generation"!'

Emma Kniebe, Children's Pastor, Holy Trinity Clapham

The Now Generation

Empowering People to Lead and Have Influence Today

Andy Monks

instant
apostle

First published in Great Britain in 2023

Instant Apostle
104 The Drive
Rickmansworth
Herts
WD3 4DU

if notified, will formally seek permission at the earliest opportunity.

The views and opinions expressed in this work are those of the author and do not necessarily reflect the views and opinions of the publisher.

British Library Cataloguing-in-Publication Data

A catalogue record for this book is available from the British Library.

This book and all other Instant Apostle books are available from Instant Apostle:

Website: www.instantapostle.com

Email: info@instantapostle.com

ISBN 978-1-912726-66-0

Printed in Great Britain.

This book is dedicated to the
Youth at Christ Church Aughton.

I wrote this book *for* you and *because* of you. Thank you
for inspiring every page of this book and teaching me
what it looks like to be in an environment where
everyone truly is valued.

I will never forget every adventure we went on together.

#GreaterThings

Contents

Foreword 13

Introduction: Now Is the Time 15

Part One: Definitions 23

    1: Leaders Are Ships 25

    2: Leaders Are Elevators 32

    3: Leaders Are Greenhouses 39

Part Two: Learning to Lead 49

    4: Taking the First Step 51

    5: Gaining Experience 56

    6: Mistakes Happen 63

    7: Working on Your Weakness 69

    8: Do Something Different 77

    9: Unseen Results 83

    10: Listen to the Right Voices 91

Part Three: Taking the Lead 99

  11: Putting Yourself Out There 101

  12: Leaving an Effective Legacy 108

  13: Bossing Time Management 115

  14: Understanding the Power of 'No' 123

  15: Own the Moment 131

  16: Facing Opposition 139

  17: Communication Skills 146

Part Four: Helping Others to Lead 155

  18: Taking Others on the Journey 157

  19: Know Your People 165

  20: Baggage vs Luggage 172

  21: Practical Beats Theory 180

  22: The Value of Mentoring 185

  23: Get Out of the Way! 193

Conclusion: Never Finished 201

Foreword

I was a most reluctant leader. I moved with trepidation from being self-employed for twenty years to leading a national company with more than 800 employees. Age and experience are marvellous things. They prune your ego, they teach you to pick your battles and they teach you above all things that to lead well is fundamentally to serve well.

I have seen Andy serve with grace in his ministry and have seen how it has changed the lives around him. It is, then, leadership indeed that he took the time and energy to draw together his wisdom and learning to create this book.

For those at the threshold of leadership, wondering what that may look like, the succinct and nutritious guidance in this book will act as a Sherpa to those ordained to lead. This is a book for the reluctant leader, the timid leader, the leader who feels unworthy. Those are often the ones chosen to be beacons of hope, to create endless momentum, to be role models, to be the ones who are humble enough to constantly shrug the glory in the direction of the Leading Light. Andy Monks is a great example of such a beacon, and this fine slicing of the art of leadership is timelessly brilliant.

Nisha Katona MBE, CEO/Founder Mowgli Street Food Restaurants

Introduction
Now Is the Time

Don't let anyone think less of you because you are
young. Be an example to all believers in what you
say, in the way you live, in your love, your faith,
and your purity.
(1 Timothy 4:12, NLT)

It's fair to say, my primary school football team wasn't very good. We had lost every single game of the season and, to make matters worse, we hadn't even scored a single goal. Actually, it was even worse than that, because our team wasn't even the 'A' team, we were the 'B' team – you know, the kids who just get a game because the school is kind enough to create a second team – but deep down everyone knows you aren't *really* that good; you're in the 'B' team for a reason. So, coming into that last game of the season, no one was particularly expectant of a positive result.

The usual ending to a game was the referee blowing his whistle, the opposition celebrating and our team crying owing to the fact that we had been thumped 6-0. We would then wander back to the changing room to get out of our smelly and muddy kit. In the process of getting changed, you would be more than likely to see most of us sulking, while the rest of the team hurled insults and blame at each other; the occasional muddy sock was also thrown. Sadly, I participated in all of these post-match acts of blame-shifting and disappointment.

At ten years old I was a very angry and very negative boy. On the pitch, I made sure others knew when they had made a mistake and I was hot-tempered when things didn't go the way I wanted. Believe it or not, I was actually the captain of the team; although, at that time, I clearly didn't tick any of the usual boxes to be classed as a good leader.

However, things in that department did begin to change.

After our team's second-to-last game of the season, where we faced the usual battering, team arguments and general negativity, my dad decided to talk to me during our car journey back home.

'You need to change,' Dad said to me. 'You are supposed to be the captain and leader of this team, but all you are doing is speaking negatively about everyone. *Good leaders don't make other people feel bad for their mistakes; they help people overcome them.*'

At the time I was so mad at everyone for how the team was performing, that this talking-to by my dad was not what I wanted. In my head, my dad should have been on my side; he should have been blaming everyone just as much as I was. Thankfully, though, my dad knew better than I did, and what he said next changed my entire life: 'At the next match, this is what I want you to do: every time you open your mouth to speak, only let good things come out. *Make everything you say be positive.* And don't stop talking!'

I listened to what my dad said and I thought to myself, 'Well, we are getting walloped every week and none of the team actually like each other, so I may as well give it a go. We've got nothing to lose.'

The final game of the season came around and within a matter of minutes we were losing 3-0. Usually, we would have conceded a goal and then given up trying for the rest of the game. Not today! This wasn't the same old story; it was a different game altogether. We kept going! In fact, we were relentless.

My dad's advice was right, and I could hear it ringing in my ears throughout the match. I didn't shut up all game and all the words that left my mouth were filled with positivity and encouragement (actually, there was one moment I phrased something negatively, which my dad heard; he glared at me. Needless to say, I wasn't going to do that again!).

You know what? It was incredible to see first-hand how speaking with positivity could change the environment around me.

As the game continued, our team's efforts remained as high as possible. In the end, we got our reward, a moment I will never forget. There was a boy in our team who was capable of producing a long, looping throw-in and we had been given a chance for him to utilise this ability. I remember him throwing the ball in, my legs running as fast as they could towards the ball, the ball colliding with my head and then flying past the goalkeeper into the back of the net. We had scored! Everyone was absolutely buzzing! The whole team all piled on top of me in celebration; it was a special moment for every single one of us.

The game finally came to an end with us losing 7-2. Yet the defeat didn't matter to us; we were bouncing with positivity and the fact we had managed to score two goals – our first two goals as a team. Seeing everyone so happy and encouraging each other in the changing rooms afterwards was magical; our team had truly been transformed through better leadership – we even folded our kit away neatly back inside the kitbag. Although, the best part of the post-match hype for me was walking off the pitch at the end of the game, and seeing my dad smiling at me; his face beaming, his eyes looking at me softly and with gentleness. I knew straight away that he was proud of the positive leadership he had witnessed that day.

There were many lessons I learned from this experience; I learned what it meant to lead properly, to bring the best out of others, to inject positivity into a team, and I truly learned how 'leadership is influence'.[1] However, the biggest and probably most important lesson was that *you are never too young to be a leader.*

This is the message behind this book.

In today's society, whether that be in the media, sport, business or the Church, the term 'the next generation' is often used to describe young people. This phrase implies that young people will be the leaders of the future – which they most certainly will! However, it also limits the impact

---

[1] John Maxwell, *The 21 Irrefutable Law of Leadership* (Nashville, TN: Thomas Nelson, 1998), p 11.

young people can have on the world, as it implies that today, the here and now, is not the time for young people to lead.

Personally, I do not believe that this is true, or that this limiting language is what God would use to describe the young people He has created. God has gifted young people and He has called them to set an example to others, in many different ways, as it says in 1 Timothy 4:12. Therefore, God has placed things within young people to do this, so they can impact the world *today*, not just *tomorrow* as the phrase 'the next generation' suggests. As a result, I am certain that young people should not be called 'the next generation', but rather they should be empowered as *the now generation* because now is the time for young people to step up, lead and positively influence the world. It's time to rewrite the narrative.

As someone who had his first job in leadership at thirteen years old, I can testify to being part of *the now generation* and having influence from a young age. Throughout this book I will share my experiences of being a leader as a young person. In sharing my story, illustrating pictures of leadership and offering some general tips of application, my prayer and hope is that you would see that you are someone who is able to lead and have influence on the world and those around you today. *You don't need to wait for tomorrow; now can be the time to start the journey of leadership*, no matter how young you are.

To help you progress on your journey of leadership and influence, this book will be split into sections:

1. **Definitions**. This section will identify and define what leadership is. Through this section, we will see how

leadership is not merely about holding a position, but is about having positive influence and impact on those around you.

2. **Learning to Lead**. Whenever you start anything new there are always lots of lessons to learn. The 'Learning to Lead' section will help you take hold and make the most of every opportunity that comes your way. This will also show you how it is important to be nurtured by others and how to go about learning from people further along the journey than yourself.

3. **Taking the Lead**. As you continue to progress in life and in leadership, it is natural that you will gain more responsibility as time goes on. The 'Taking the Lead' section will show you how to steward this responsibility well and to work effectively as part of a team.

4. **Helping Others to Lead**. The best thing any leader can do is make more leaders. This section will show you how to take others with you on the journey of leadership and help them reach their own full potential, maximising the positive influence on the world.

I wrote this book with the aim of demonstrating how you can lead as a young person. Regardless of what you may have heard or the discouragement you may have received, everyone can lead and be a person of influence – including you! This book is about helping you take the steps to become the best possible version of yourself, in order to reach your full God-given potential and have the greatest influence in every sphere of society, relationship and interaction that you find yourself in. Through this book, I hope you too will see that you are a part of *the now generation*, and that no matter what your age, you are someone who can bring influence, have fun and leave a legacy. Today!

Now is your time...

Part One
Definitions

Definitions are important in many areas of life, including leadership. One of the main reasons why people can often feel like they are not a leader is because they have a wrong definition and understanding of what it actually means to be a leader. This opening section will provide you with a number of pictorial definitions of leadership, which will show you how everyone is a leader – including you!

1
Leaders Are Ships

*In every interaction with someone, you are always
leading them somewhere.*

When you think of a leader, what sort of person do you
think of? Perhaps you may think about those in
government who have the huge responsibility of leading
a country, or you may think about your teachers and
coaches who have helped you to learn in school, or you
could think about those people who stand on stages in
front of crowds of people and give talks. Whoever you
have thought about, it is likely that they are in a formal
position of leadership and probably get paid to lead a
group of people and do what they do.

However, leadership is not merely about position. Just
because someone holds a particular position or status does
not always guarantee that they are a good leader. On the
other hand, even if someone does not hold a particular
position, it does not mean they are not a leader.
Leadership is about influence. *Having influence on another
person has nothing to do with your position, but has everything
to do with your relationship.*

The reality is that everyone has influence, every day.

Every day you will have an impact on other people – even in what may seem like the most simple, normal and ordinary of ways. For example, if two friends meet up for a coffee and have a conversation, they will leave the conversation thinking one of two things: that the conversation was a positive experience, or that it was a negative one. *This is because, in every interaction with someone, you are always leading them somewhere.*

Recently, I met with my friend Caz for a coffee and a chat. We had an incredible time together! There was laughter and there were terrific, deep, meaningful aspects to the conversation. As a result, I left my time with Caz feeling great. But if Caz had spent the whole conversation on her phone and had not been interested in anything I had to say, I would have left our time together feeling very disheartened.

You see, this is how simple leadership and influence is. Caz was just being a friend to me as we spent time together, but there was something much greater going on: she was having positive influence on my life.

Leadership really is that simple. *Leadership is not about position, but positive influence.*

In looking at this simplicity of leadership it is clear that there is a big emphasis on friendship and relationship to bring positive influence. You could also say that the same is the case with discipleship, as it can happen in the everyday of life through our normal interactions with others who follow Jesus.

Interestingly, if you look at the four key words in those sentences …

- Leadership
- Friendship
- Relationship
- Discipleship

… you will see something that each of these words have in common. Can you see it? Yes, they all have the word *ship* at the end. As we look to give pictorial definitions of leadership in this opening section, the first picture we are going to look at is how *leaders* are *ships*.

Personally, I don't have much experience in, on or around ships, unlike my grandfather, who spent much of his early life living on various ships. He was a radio officer for the Merchant Navy, meaning he spent much of his working life travelling on ships to many various parts of the world. There were so many great stories he had to share with us as a family about all the places he had visited, as well as the people he worked with. As I reflected on my grandfather's stories and experiences, it was clear to me that there were key characteristics and functions of the ship that are also key characteristics in positive leadership.

1. Direction on the journey

As I said, my grandfather would tell us about all the different places he had visited while in the Merchant Navy. However, it was talking about the ships themselves that gave my grandfather the greatest joy. This was because he spent more time at sea on the ships than he did on dry land. My grandfather would remind us that if it were not for the ships fulfilling their purpose, he would not have had the opportunity to reach the many different parts of the globe that he did.

Leaders do exactly the same. *Leaders take you on a journey and help you reach places and purposes you wouldn't reach without them.* There are so many people I can think of who have done this for me during my own life – many of these *ships* you will hear about throughout this book – though the principle at play here is that no matter who you are, you can always take others on a journey. Again, any relationship and friendship will see this happen. So no matter what your age, you are never too young to journey through life with others and help them on their way to reaching where they need to be – even if that is just helping them with one step.

2. Emphasis on teamwork

Naturally, because relationships play such a huge part in having a positive influence on others, teamwork is also of high significance. One of the things that made life on the ships so memorable for my grandfather was the people he shared the events with – in other words, these people led him to have many positive experiences.

If you ever watch a movie that includes pirates and a pirate ship, one of the things you will notice is how the pirates always work together – even if it is for unlawful reasons! OK, I know there is the occasional mutiny, but when there is good leadership at the helm, the pirates pull together as a team to work towards a shared goal... or the promise of treasure.

Even though you and those you interact with may not be pirates, all of us need people to help us on the journey of life. Very early on in the Bible, even God says, 'It is not good for the man to be alone' (Genesis 2:18). Whether we like it or not, *we all need people*; we were designed by God, for relationship with Him and with others. We truly are better together. There are people who need you in their life, to be the *ship* that they need, and vice versa. After all, everyone needs a helping hand from time to time. This is where teamwork really comes into its own. So have confidence in yourself. You can bring people together and have a positive influence on a group.

One of the common things you will see in leaders who are *ships* is their ability to bring people together. I am sure you can all name people in your friendship groups who do this. For example, they are usually the first person in your group chats to suggest getting together at the weekend. They often come up with good activities that you may be able to do as a group and they are the ones who will be willing to speak up and make a decision when no one else in the group has the confidence to do so. Whatever the case, these people bring the group closer together, creating a place for relationships to grow and blossom.

3. Protection through the storm

Finally, as part of bringing direction to people's journey through life and allowing people to be part of a team, leaders who are *ships* will also carry people through the storms of life. Sadly, life is not always perfect and it is inevitable that storms will arise from time to time – you will see this through some of my experiences. Leaders are not exempt from the storms of life and need to know how to guide themselves and others through them.

Thankfully, ships are very helpful in storms. They provide protection and are designed to withstand the harshest of conditions to carry those on board to the golden skies, calm waters and bright beaches that await on the other side of the storm. Friends are great at this!

As I have tried to portray in this chapter, leadership plays a part in the everydayness of life and this occurs naturally through ordinary, day-to-day relationships. And when it comes to storms, friends are the best people to help lead anyone to the peace-filled waters on the other side.

This is because good friends will listen well, give sound advice when needed, and stay close throughout the stormy season. I'm sure everyone has been on both sides of this scenario. When you are that friend who plays the role of being the steady base of support for someone in the midst of their storm, you are being the *leader*, and the *ship* that they need to carry them through.

Everyone can do this, because leadership happens in the everyday and is for everyone.

Summary: *Leadership happens in the everyday activities and normality of life. In every interaction you can lead someone to either a positive experience or a negative experience. Being a leader who is like a ship means you can always take people on a journey, bring forth opportunities for open communication, and are a support for people when the inevitable storms of life arise.*

2
Leaders Are Elevators

Sometimes you have to go down to go up.

If you look back at your life, would you be honest enough to say that you remember certain situations, events or moments better than others? For some reason, there are particular chapters of life (and Netflix episodes) that seem to stick in the mind more than others.

Personally, I love looking back at my life and seeing how far I have come; but I must admit, sometimes there are certain details I seem to remember, yet I have no idea why. These memories are not of big events, they are not of life-changing experiences and they are not even of great revelations from God. In many ways they consist of absolutely pointless memories. So pointless that it makes no sense as to why the brain would want to latch on to these memories in the first place; let alone store them up in the long-term memory bank. How it is possible for them to have made the cut, to have journeyed from my short-term memory to my long-term memory ahead of other, potentially more important and significant memories, I will never know or fully understand.

One of these memories is from a family holiday to Salou, in Spain, when I was around the age of ten. I was with my family, enjoying the sunshine and the freedom of playing with new friends I had made around our hotel pool. Then, all of a sudden, I realised that I had left something of importance in our hotel room. Funnily enough, the only aspect of this story I cannot remember is what exactly I had forgotten to pick up from the room. So I went back inside the hotel to get whatever important item I had left behind.

The hotel room we were staying in was on one of the top floors of the hotel, meaning I had to take the elevator to get up there. Now, here comes my pointless, lasting memory that I have never been able to shake – the elevator itself. Yep, it was one incredible elevator!

The doors and the inside of the elevator possessed a beautiful marble décor. The buttons on the console were a high-quality plastic which looked brand new, and they sat in their place, with purple neon lights. These neon lights also surrounded the edges of the elevator walls, one of which had a pristine mirror on it, which was so clear it was as if you could look into it and see beneath the layers of your own skin. This elevator was amazing; it was beautiful.

It's fascinating how an elevator has lodged itself in my long-term memory and refuses to leave. Yet I believe this is the same with leaders and those people we meet throughout our time on earth who have had a big influence on our lives. When someone influences you in such positive ways, it is hard to prevent them entering the long-term memory bank. They are the people who have helped mould you into who you are today, they have been there for you when no one else was and they are the people who give you pieces of wisdom that are absolute game-changers as to how you decide to live your life.

They are the elevators in your life. They are people who are influentially, unequivocally, unforgettable.

As part of *the now generation*, you too can be an elevator in the lives of others. There are key features that make up an elevator which leaders also possess in order to have positive influence on the lives of others. Here they are:

1. Open doors

Before stepping into an elevator, the doors must be opened to allow you passage inside. Similarly, leaders make it a habit to open doors for other people. The best leaders often have an 'it's not about me' mentality. Meaning, it is all about others and the people they are serving; it is not about themselves. As a result, leaders love to give others opportunities. This could be by creating space for people to speak in group situations, such as during meetings. Additionally, a leader may use their areas of influence and relationships to enable someone to have an opportunity to do an activity for the first-ever time. Both of these work towards the goal of empowering people with a sense of purpose, value and belonging within the group, and so increasing the influence of the individual and the whole team.

My brother Mark is fantastic when it comes to opening doors! He makes it his mission to open as many doors for people as he can each and every day. By the way, when I say doors, I mean literal doors. You could say that Mark is being a kind and considerate gentleman (or butler-in-training) by holding doors open for others, but I think it is a vital skill that every leader requires, regardless of what point in their own leadership journey they are currently at.

As I write this, Mark is still in his teenage years and is only just about to start his GCSEs. But why should that prevent him, or anyone for that matter, from being a door opener? It shouldn't! With humility and a heart to serve others, anyone can be a door opener. I believe this habitual skill will stick with Mark for a lifetime – and I hope it does. I hope there are many leaders who can learn to be door openers, because *no one can be elevated without someone first opening a door for them.*

2. Provide a platform to stand on

After the door to an elevator opens, you will naturally move into the elevator and stand inside it. The place where you stand is a platform. This platform is a safe space for someone to stand. It is a place that those who enter the elevator trust will support their weight as they move up or down the floor levels.

Leaders will also create platforms for people. This may be through putting someone in a position to use their gifting or present something that they feel is on their heart. Whatever the platform is for, it will allow someone to be fully themselves, while helping them to grow at the same time – especially as, at first, someone may feel uncomfortable when standing on the platform. However, it is vitally important that these platforms are safe and that those standing on them know it, believe it and trust in it.

Someone would not follow a leader unless they felt and knew wholeheartedly that the leader would be there to support them – just as an elevator supports a person's weight.

3. Push the right buttons

Once someone is standing on the platform inside the elevator, they will then push the appropriate button to get to the level that they need. Sometimes the elevator will go up; sometimes it will go down. It all depends on what button has been pressed. But in order for the elevator to move, you have to push the button.

I am sure we all have people in our lives who have (or still do) pushed our buttons – or simply annoy us. This could be seen as both a positive and a negative thing when it comes to leadership, and it can be annoying to have someone push your buttons. However, to get the best out of someone, there are times when buttons may have to be pressed. A good leader will know the best timing and the best method to do this.

I particularly remember one teacher I had in secondary school. He was the school sports coach and boy, oh boy, did he know how to push my buttons! At the time I thought he was just saying things to me for the sake of being cheeky and extremely annoying. Looking back, though, I can see how this actually was not the case. Upon reviewing all of my performances in cricket over the years, that year was by far the best I had. So, in actual fact, that teacher was being a good leader, because he knew what I needed to hear in order to elevate my levels of performance.

The buttons that bring the best out of each person will be different; but good leaders bring the best out of people, because they know which buttons *to* press and which buttons *not to* press. If my school teacher/coach used the same tactics to get the best out of other people on the team it might not have worked, as we are all different; but what I saw from that teacher was how he got the best out of everyone, as he knew which buttons needed to be pressed with each person because he took the time to learn each player's personality and individuality.

It is worth noting here that pushing the right buttons is not always about *elevation*. Elevators are designed to go up and down. Sometimes, the best thing a leader can do for someone is take them down a level or two. It is in this 'pushing the right button' approach that a leader will position someone at the most appropriate level they need at a given moment, in order to produce their best performance in the long run.

For example, my school coach would often make me work on specific drills in training. These drills often seemed tedious, repetitive and a little bit too basic. At times I would feel like I was being treated like a child, being taught the basics over and over again. Despite my initial frustrations, however, I soon began to notice a greater level of consistency in my cricket performance. Going back down a level, as my coach had instructed, made such a huge difference. *Never underestimate the effectiveness of going back to the basics.* Sometimes, you have to go down before you can go up.

An effective leader will be the kind of elevator who gets people to the level they need – whether that's through going up or going down.

***Summary:** Leaders want to see others become the best version of themselves, fulfil their potential and make a difference wherever they are in the world. As a result, leaders will do all they can to elevate others by creating opportunities for them, giving them a platform and pushing the appropriate buttons to produce their best.*

3
Leaders Are Greenhouses

Good leaders are like greenhouses; things grow in their presence.

In the summer of 2020, I remember when we, in England, experienced our first easing of the COVID-19 lockdown. Part of this easing meant that it was possible to visit someone in their garden. In going to see people, there was something that you could not help but notice. It was very evident as to which people had spent time looking after their gardens in lockdown and those who had let things get a bit out of hand.

I remember when I went to see a young person from our church youth group who had evidently spent many an hour in their garden during the lockdown. The grass looked lush green and was shaded just like a football pitch, the flowers were bright in their colours, and this person had even dug themselves an allotment plot to grow their own vegetables.

Unlike this young person, I am not so active in the garden, unless it involves shooting basketball hoops with my brother Mark. However, if you are a leader, then you are called to be like a gardener, just like in the Bible passage found in Mark 4 about a farmer who went out into the field and scattered seed. Like the farmer, we also should scatter as much seed as possible, as the seed represents the Word of God, which brings positive influence like nothing else can.

In this Bible parable, there is a clear distinction between the locations in which the seed will land: on the hard ground where it is eaten by the birds, in the rocky places where it can't take root, among the thorns where the seed is choked, or in the good soil where it can grow and produce a crop. Our prayer as leaders is that all seed we sow will land on good soil, but sadly this is not always the case – hence the need to scatter a lot of seed.

Furthermore, for the seed that does land on the good soil, we want to see that seed grow into its full potential – although it is important to note that for any seed to grow into its full potential it needs to be in the right environment.

Sometimes, you will see people who have a greenhouse in their garden. My grandfather was a very keen greenhouse user when it came to spring and summer, as each year he would use it to help grow his tomato plants. I remember many times turning up at his house to find him working out there. As I went to see him working on his tomato plants, I would often ask him why he chose to grow his plants in the greenhouse rather than outside.

There were many reasons stated by my grandfather, but what I have realised as I have got older is that there are similarities between what a greenhouse does for plants and what good leaders do for people. Simply put, a greenhouse is designed to support plant growth in a nurturing and caring environment. The same applies to leaders, as they try to cultivate a healthy space for other people to develop and reach their full potential.

Good leaders are like greenhouses; things grow in their presence. Where a greenhouse causes a plant to grow, good leaders cause people to grow. Both are catalysts for growth, because they create an environment for the right ingredients to merge together and cause growth as a result.

This growth of plants, and people, can occur through optimising three particular aspects:

1. Optimal content

If you think about the times you learned about plants in school, I'm sure there is one word that naturally springs to mind: photosynthesis. Photosynthesis explains a process that employs these ingredients: water, sunlight and carbon dioxide. Without these three elements, plants would not grow. If used in the right way, a greenhouse can produce the right environment to maximise the effect of these three natural resources.

In the area of leadership, growing people is not as straightforward as growing plants. Where most plants will simply need the three elements of photosynthesis, the necessary elements for personal growth of each individual can be varied – people are different and therefore their needs are different. As a result, one key ability a good leader possesses is the ability to detect what will bring optimal growth to a specific individual.

Jesus modelled this perfectly. In all of the stories or metaphors He used, He used language that the audience present would have understood. For example, when a woman went to her usual well in John 4 to collect water, Jesus spoke to her about water. From reading John 4 we see how Jesus' choice of content brought forth life, transformational change and growth for this woman, because Jesus knew her individual needs in order to attain optimum growth. Therefore, a leader needs to be a greenhouse that is adaptable, to create the optimal content required for an individual person. In doing so, the leader will maximise the influence they can have when particular people cross their path.

2. Optimal temperature

If you have ever stepped into a greenhouse on a particularly hot sunny day, I can guarantee your first reaction will have been somewhere along the lines of, 'Oh my days, it's hot in here!' That's because one of the abilities a greenhouse has is to trap heat. This helps plants to grow owing to the increased humidity. The natural moisture formed as a result of this heat is then used by the plant, as a contributing factor to photosynthesis.

Basically, a plant sweats, and that sweat is then taken in as a water source by the plant. Therefore, the optimal temperature of a greenhouse causes the plant to sweat to the appropriate level required to produce growth at a more efficient speed.

In regard to leadership, it is often said that people don't grow to their full potential while in their comfort zone. In greenhouse terms, some heat needs to be applied to produce some *sweat* that will then produce growth in the plant. Of course, the *temperature* applied has to be at the optimal level for the individual you are investing in. People are different, so will respond differently to different levels of pressure being applied to them – a bit like knowing how to appropriately push someone's buttons, as we said earlier.

One way we have tried to do this in our church youth group is through a simple exercise, which we call 'The Ring of Fire'. The idea and primary purpose of this exercise is to help prepare the young people for facing situations where pressure is applied by their peers who may ask hard questions about their faith or life. 'The Ring of Fire' is set up to replicate these scenarios, while demonstrating what it means to not 'worry about what to say or how to say it. At that time, you will be given what to say, for it will not be you speaking, but the Spirit of your Father speaking through you' (Matthew 10:19-20).

In this exercise, a young person will be given a random word, which they then have to speak on for thirty seconds and try to find some link to faith, with literally no time to prepare.

At first, every member of the group was apprehensive about this activity; however, once they had completed their thirty seconds of speaking, all of the young people reported that they used words and phrases that they would never normally have thought to use. Furthermore, they all responded positively to the exercise, saying how they felt something had been 'activated' within them. They also desired to do this exercise more as they felt an immediate growth and strengthening of their faith muscles. Owing to the highly enthusiastic response, similar exercises are now used on a regular basis.

The point to make here is, although the young people may have been taken somewhat out of their comfort zone and they may have *felt the heat*, there was clear growth in all of them. Just like a plant in the greenhouse, the temperature was optimal for the growth they needed in the moment.

3. Optimal exposure

Finally, a greenhouse creates an environment of optimal exposure. Simply put, a greenhouse creates an environment where a plant will receive the optimal content and temperature, at the optimal level of exposure it requires. For example, when it comes to the amount of light required in the process of photosynthesis, a greenhouse has an amplifying effect on the light. This increases a plant's exposure to the amount of light it receives, which will, again, aid the growth of the plant.

On the other hand, a greenhouse also has a protective quality about it. Living in Britain, we are all too familiar with wet and wild summers. I know for myself, it is not uncommon to see tree branches that have gone astray in the middle of roads, or in the back garden, as a result of the typically windy and wet weather of the British summer.

With all this going on, there is potential damage that could be caused to a plant placed outdoors – extreme rain could drown the plant and high winds could pull the plant's roots out of the ground. A greenhouse provides protection from these elements, meaning the plant is not overexposed.

In leading people, allowing the right exposure is also key. *Exposure is necessary for growth, but overexposure can be destructive.* The best analogy I have come across, with regard to finding the right exposure for people to grow, is 'tightropes and safety nets'.[2] The picture created here is one of stepping out of your comfort zone, while being safe at the same time. As stepping out onto a tightrope seems daunting, yet knowing there is a safety net there to catch you if you fall is very reassuring and helps you to feel safe.

Recently, there was a guy in our church who I felt God was calling to speak for the very first time. I spoke to him about it. He was very willing, but he said he felt anxious, owing to it being his first time and with the level of exposure that comes with speaking in front of a group of people. So, I put forward the idea that we could do the talk together, tag-team style – meaning I would speak some parts, he would speak some parts and we would flow between ourselves in a natural way. This enabled him to feel supported in stepping onto the tightrope and, more importantly, it meant that if at any point during the talk he got stuck or lost his bearings, I was there as the safety net to catch him and fill in if required.

Jesus himself also modelled this approach in leadership. Of course, while thinking about stepping out, it's easy to link this to Peter stepping out of the boat and walking on water from Matthew 14:22-33. As Jesus asked Peter to step out, it was as if he was inviting Peter onto that

---

[2] Pete Wynter (director of Leadership College London and vicar of St Paul's Hammersmith), quote from seminar on leadership at the Youthscape 'National Youth Ministry Weekend' conference, 16th November 2019. Youthscape is an organisation that invests into youth leaders – www.youthscape.co.uk (accessed 8 August 2022).

tightrope – although having said that, I think stepping onto water is next-level stuff compared to a tightrope. Anyway, no matter how uncomfortable Peter may have felt, Jesus was there, ready to catch him.

People grow when taken out of their comfort zone, but it's unlikely that growth will occur if there are too many negative emotions going on within them. Hence the need for the safety net. It allows people to feel stretched without feeling overexposed to the point where they are going to break. That is the optimal exposure to produce growth.

So leading like a greenhouse produces the optimal environment for people to grow. However, there is one thing that must be said about greenhouses before we finish this 'definitions' section. Greenhouses are expensive. It costs to have them installed in the first place and then it costs even more to maintain them over time. You could view this as a disadvantage, although, if you have been in leadership for any considerable length of time, I'm sure you would say that it's worth the cost of investment. Furthermore, the cost of maintaining a greenhouse, or maintaining yourself, is essential, because *if a greenhouse isn't in optimal condition itself, it can't create the optimal environment for things to grow inside it.* Therefore, the costs are not a disadvantage but a privilege, as the reward of watching people reach their full potential is far greater than the cost itself.

Finally, although there is a cost to maintaining a greenhouse, there is also one great benefit. A greenhouse allows you to sow seeds earlier and reap for longer, increasing the level of influence that is possible. Because of the properties we have mentioned, a greenhouse can optimise growth so much that it can bring it early in spring and late into the summer.

Therefore, if you want to be a leader who is like a greenhouse, with the optimal content, temperature and exposure:

> Preach the word; *be prepared in season and out of season*; correct, rebuke and encourage – with great patience and careful instruction.
> (2 Timothy 4:2, my emphasis)

Summary: *Leaders create the optimal environment for people to grow. Although they need to invest highly to see this growth occur, leaders know that the outcome of people growing is of far greater value than any cost they could have incurred through the process.*

Part summary

Through this first part of the book, we have seen how leadership is not about holding a position or title, but rather it is about having positive influence on those around you. This can happen in everyday life through any relationship that we have. In doing so, we can be a ship that takes people on a journey, an elevator that opens doors for people, and a greenhouse that creates a space for others to grow to their optimal level. As we continue through this book, hold on to these three pictures and see how they are at play within every story and every lesson of leadership that follows.

Part Two
Learning to Lead

Now that we know what leadership is all about, we can look at how we can start to become the best leader possible. One of the most important things to remember with leadership, and a lot of other aspects of life, is that it is a process – a process of learning. Learning comes through taking opportunities and gaining experience. This section will show you the benefits of taking these opportunities and demonstrate how the experiences you gain will help you learn to lead. No matter how long you have or haven't been a leader, this section is essential, because the process of learning is never finished.

4
Taking the First Step

The hardest step of the journey is often the first
one.

In conjunction with playing lots of football, swimming was the other main sport I participated in as a child. I loved it; at one point I was even training three times a week. There was something about the water that just made me feel great. Personally, I think this was because my mum took me to baby swimming classes from the age of three months, but there could have been many other reasons. Either way, the water felt like home to me.

Furthermore, the people I trained with were absolute top quality and the banter was electric. In fact, the banter in the boys' changing room after training sessions was so free-flowing that the girls would always have finished getting changed while we were still only just getting out of our swimming kits! Being involved in the sport of swimming wasn't just about swimming; it was about friendship.

As time progressed, me and my friend Chris became among the oldest people to be swimming at the club.

Because of this, the owners of the swimming club asked us if we fancied a go at trying to teach, because they thought it was an appropriate step towards our continued development.

When presented with an opportunity like this, there are many different thoughts that go through your mind, especially as a young person. There are the positive and encouraging thoughts that someone first of all noticed you, let alone that they could think of you upholding such a great position and responsibility. However, there are also the negative thoughts that can enter your mind. You could feel afraid. Afraid of failure and letting others down, afraid of suffering with the load that comes with leadership, or afraid of possible conflict with those you are working with and leading. Ultimately, though, all fear is underlined by the biggest fear – that we aren't good enough.[3]

For me, when asked to start swimming teaching, it was a vast mixture of positive and negative thoughts and emotions. I was thrilled to be asked to be a teacher: what a privilege, especially at thirteen! But at the same time, I was definitely terrified that I wouldn't be good enough. At the end of the day, those who were teaching me made it look so effortless and, in my head, getting to that sort of level seemed an impossible feat.

Despite my mixed emotions, I said 'Yes' to the opportunity to teach swimming; as did Chris, which was a real blessing, as it meant we would be learning the art of teaching together. Although, to get to the point of saying

[3] See Ant Middleton, *The Fear Bubble* (London: HarperCollins, 2020), p 290.

yes, I did have to battle with those negative thoughts and self-talk. The only way I was able to overcome this battle was to put a positive spin on everything. Similar to what my dad said to me about the football team, I had to talk to myself positively. This is essential when deciding to take a new opportunity, because *talking positively will talk you into something while talking negatively will talk you out of it.*

So when facing these moments where a new opportunity presents itself and your mind wants to tell you nothing but negatives, here are some positive truths to think about and remind yourself of. These helped me to take the first step in saying yes to becoming a swimming teacher.

1. You have value

Every person on the planet is valuable. That includes you!

The main reason why Jesus came to earth was because 'God so loved the world that he gave his one and only Son' (John 3:16). Jesus died on the cross for every single one of us. We are all seen with equal value in His eyes; His love for each and every one of us is the same and given unconditionally with grace. Therefore, we can always be reassured that our performance does not change God's love for us.

When interviewed by Sky Sports News, the director of Christians in Sport, Graham Daniels, stated how one of the reasons why the world has such a mental health crisis is because there is such high pressure on people to perform, whereas all people really want is to be loved regardless of the quality of their performance.[4] God's love epitomises this point – *regardless of your performance you are loved and valued!*

Furthermore, if you ever doubt yourself when being offered a new opportunity, it is always worth remembering that *you* were the person asked. Someone would not offer you an opportunity unless they saw something in you that they valued. *There are moments where people can see something inside you which you might not be able to see yourself.* Trust the value people see in you and believe that it is true, because it could lead you into something amazing. I'm glad I decided to trust what the leaders of my swimming club saw in me, because becoming a swimming teacher was a pivotal moment in my life.

2. Don't expect too much of yourself

There are many people who say 'No' to opportunities because they either expect too much of themselves or compare themselves to someone else. Of course, it is very possible to do both of these at the same time. When it comes to opportunities for things you have never done before, there should actually be no performance-based expectations upon you. After all, this is something you have never done before, so how can you expect so much with no experience? Furthermore, when it comes to comparison, how can you compare yourself to someone who has years of experience when you don't have any? It doesn't make sense. *The only person you should compare*

---

[4] Christians in Sport, www.youtube.com/watch?v=Vsqo2AkpPnQ (accessed 8th May 2020).

yourself to is the person you were yesterday; but only to see how much you have grown.

All forms of disappointment come from having unmet expectations.[5] If we look back at the angry version of young me from the introduction, the cause of all my frustration was unmet expectation. I expected my team to be the best team in the world, not a school 'B' team made up of nine- and ten-year-old boys. It would have been impossible for our team to achieve the level of expectation I had placed on them.

So when you take that first step, don't put too much expectation on yourself, and don't compare yourself to others; rather, see yourself as a blank canvas with endless possibilities. Saying yes is the start of the masterpiece.

Summary: *The journey into leadership and influence starts by saying yes! When given an opportunity to step into leadership, believe that you have value and don't expect too much of yourself. Say 'Yes', take it one step at a time and trust that the best is yet to come!*

---

[5] Mike Todd talk 'Rip Up Your List'.
www.youtube.com/watch?v=88TTZgPrtko (accessed 3rd May 2020).

5
Gaining Experience

Exposure produces experience. Experience leads to maturity.

Whenever you start something new, the first thing you do is learn – a lot! Thankfully for my friend Chris and me, we were in the most capable hands to teach us how to be swimming instructors. We had Richard. Richard was a legend on the poolside – everyone who had a lesson with Richard always noted how they had improved technically. For years that was Chris and me. We were in Richard's class every week and we were fully aware of every reason why Richard was the best around.

Richard was a slim and very tall man, with a beaming smile that went from ear to ear. He was a very calm and humble man, too, who truly valued people and moved himself in a gentle and elegant fashion. You felt at ease being around Richard, especially after he told you a joke. Richard told absolutely terrible jokes; he had a brand-new Christmas-cracker-level joke lined up for us on arrival every week.

Richard just had a special way about him that made us feel confident in being ourselves, and he made it obvious he had a stirring passion to bring the best out of us and those we were teaching. He was brilliant, everyone looked up to him, and for the new kids on the block, Chris and I wanted to be teachers like Richard. Being given the chance to learn from him was a huge honour.

In the few months that followed, Chris and I learned from Richard while teaching the top-ability group of the swimming club. We learned the best ways to deliver instructions to swimmers, the appropriate language to use when communicating, and how to be a source of encouragement. It was great. Chris and I were developing quickly and growing in confidence as teachers with Richard's support.

However, just as we were getting going, I was given the opportunity to go and teach in a different class. I had been teaching the top-ability class with Richard, but now I was about to enter a completely different world; I was going to teach one of the beginner classes. This meant changing from teaching on the poolside to teaching in the water.

There were lots of new aspects to learn with this change of environment, which is an important thing to note with leadership and life, because *you will learn more from something new than something old.* So if you want to keep learning, one of the best things to do is embrace new experiences.

This was precisely the case with my new teaching experience. It was like starting from scratch and learning to teach all over again. All the things I had learned about communication from Richard were different here; not to mention you had to be on your toes constantly – you never

57

knew when you had to stop a kid from going under the water.

Thankfully, in this new class, I was working with Rachel, who was vastly experienced in this area and, as with Richard, learning from her was a great blessing. In fact, Rachel and I ended up working together for a number of years. It's fair to say, we complemented each other well.

Wherever you are on your leadership journey, there is always more to experience; the world is always changing and there is a never-ending wealth of possibilities available. When facing new situations and gaining further experience, it is always helpful to expose yourself to the right people and have an air of experimentation about you to discover a methodology that works for you. Here's how to go about both of these:

1. Exposure: surround yourself with people who are better than you

Proverbs 13:20 says, 'Walk with the wise and become wise, for a companion of fools suffers harm.' In simple terms, this proverb is highlighting how the people you surround yourself with will have a significant impact on your life. To phrase it differently: each person will either be an *influencer* or an *influenza* on your life – they will either make you better or make you sick.

For example, we previously said how your own self-talk will either talk you into something or out of it. This is also true for the people around you. If you expose yourself to negative people, it is likely you will also become negative. Conversely, if you surround yourself with positive thinkers, it is more likely you will also think positively.

People will rub off on you whether you like it or not. It's because of this that we end up with certain traits of our parents. As we grow up spending lots of time in an environment created by them, with their genetics running through us, it is only natural that we will pick up some of their habits.

Hence my delight as a young leader to be surrounded by the likes of Richard and Rachel. I knew they were experts in the area of swimming teaching and I wanted to be at their level. There will always be people in your life with more experience and who do things better than you. That's OK; it's normal. But what a blessing to be exposed to those further along than you, whom you can learn from.

Even as I have gotten older, I still understand the power of being in the presence of those who are better than me. Currently I work as a children's and youth worker, as does my friend Emily, although she has been in the job much longer than I have. As a result, Emily has a far greater bank of experience than me; plus, she has an exceptionally high reputation owing to her consistent success, alongside her attractive and infectious personality. She has an endless supply of good qualities, particularly in leading young people, which is exactly why I want her in my life. It is impossible for me to spend time with Emily and not have my mind stretched in some way. In a nutshell, she makes me better.

We all need people like Richard, Rachel and Emily who make us better people and better leaders. As part of *the now generation*, I pray and hope that you too can choose the right people to surround yourself with. *Choose wisely and you'll walk wisely.*

2. Experiment: be yourself and learn what works for you

One of the other things I loved about Richard was the freedom he created for me to be myself. He didn't want me to be another Richard, he wanted me to be me.

When you start out in leadership, it's natural to try to be like your role models. After all, you spend years looking up to them, viewing their successes and triumphs, so it makes sense that you would want to get in on that action.

However, you will never fully be able to be like those you look up to, or anyone else for that matter, because everyone is different. We have different personalities and thought patterns. But the fact we are all different is not a negative point; it's limitlessly beautiful – particularly with leadership. It highlights the fact that no one will ever lead in the same way, and everyone will have influence in different ways. There may be skills to pick up from others, but even in your delivery of these, it's guaranteed you'll do it differently.

Like with exam revision – I know, boring topic, but bear with me. People revise best in different ways, even though they are trying to achieve the same goal. Some like to write a lot down, some read a lot, others may talk things through. There are those who like to revise in groups, while others prefer to study independently and alone. The methods you can choose to use for revision are vast, but as I say, they are all with the aim of helping you retain information to complete an exam to the best possible standard.

Similarly, with leadership, you are always working to bring the best out of others, but each individual will have diversity in their preferred style of leadership.

Richard understood all of this, which is why he regularly encouraged us to be creative in our teaching approach. Not only that, he would often tell us to find a way that worked for us. For this to happen, Richard always made space for us to try things out. It would have been easy for him to tell us exactly what to say, how to say it, with the exact arm movements and specific facial expressions. However, this robotic approach is not sustainable in the long run.

I will never forget the moment when I was asked to take a class by myself for the very first time. This was a chance for me to use all the skills Richard had taught me, but more importantly, it was space to experiment and grow into the swimming teacher I was going to be. This did take time and there were some failures and speedbumps along the way, but it was totally worth it, as it allowed me to become a better leader, while also being myself.

In your leadership venture, don't ever be scared to be yourself and experiment with ideas to see what works for you. And if you are a leader of young people, don't be scared to release them into the space, at the right time, to be themselves.

Summary: Who you choose to put around you is important. Choose the right people and you'll become the best version of yourself. Yet, don't try too hard to become like everyone else; you were made to be you. So find ways of doing things that work best for you. The world needs you to be you.

6
Mistakes Happen

Someone who makes no mistakes does not usually make anything.[6]

In the previous chapter, we touched on the idea of experimentation within leadership. While reading this, I'm sure that some of you automatically thought of an experiment you attempted – whether that be in leadership or elsewhere. While some experiments go well, others unfortunately do not. I know for myself what it's like for an experiment not to go according to plan.

During my time in sixth form, I studied a BTEC in science, which meant that doing experiments was part of the norm. There was one particular experiment we conducted that required the use of couscous. I can't remember exactly what we were doing with the couscous, all I can remember is how the experiment went wrong.

One of the most important parts of any science experiment is safety. We were therefore required to wear safety glasses or goggles for all the experiments we did.

---

[6] Edward John Phelps, speech at Mansion House, London (24th January 1889).

On this particular occasion, though, I made the mistake of forgetting to put my glasses on, and in turn, I somehow got a piece of couscous in my eye.

I know this sounds stupid, but you have no idea how annoying and irritating that singular piece of couscous was! It was so bad that I ended up having to use the eye-washing machine (or whatever it was actually called) to try to get it out. It was very embarrassing, and my friends laughed for ages and have never let me forget about it since. Needless to say, I never forgot to put my safety goggles on again after that.

Mistakes happen in life. Mistakes happen in leadership. It's normal – you can't escape it; on some occasions you will make mistakes and get things wrong.

I never forget my first big mistake in leadership – I say big because I made many small ones. It happened when I was about fourteen and swimming teaching alongside Rachel. There was a child in our class who didn't particularly want to engage with either of us during the lessons. To be honest, I don't really think the child wanted to be there. Nevertheless, as a teacher and a leader, you always want to see anyone under your care reach their full potential.

While that sounds nice and very sincere, making that happen can feel like a long and frustrating uphill struggle. Frustration in and of itself is not always a bad thing. Commonly, it is feelings of frustration that are the starting point to innovations. For example, at the 1981 Thirsty Third World conference, leaders of the UK water industry decided to unite to find a solution to the problem of the lack of water in developing nations. This frustration was the start of the company Water Aid, which has since found solutions for millions of people to gain access to clean water sources.[7] Frustration can fuel long-term, worldwide change.

However, if frustration is not processed appropriately, it can come out in a harmful way. Sadly, this is what happened with me and the child who didn't want to engage in their swimming lessons. I got so frustrated with their lack of effort that I called them 'lazy' to try to push them to try harder. This plan dramatically failed; name-calling is not cool – as someone who got bullied himself in primary school, I can tell you first-hand that no one likes it.

I was horrified that I had allowed myself to do such a thing to anyone, let alone to a child, who became very upset. I rightly got a big telling-off from the boss. After that, I made sure that the vocabulary I used was always uplifting – *a good leader doesn't tear people apart, they build them up.* I had learned the lesson from my mistake.

We all make mistakes; it's a fact of life – they will happen. The key for all of us, especially in leadership, is to respond to making a mistake in a positive way. Here are some steps that can be taken to respond well to mistakes.

1. Accept

Once a mistake has been made, there is nothing you can do to change it. This leaves you with two choices: either you accept it has happened or you don't. If you don't accept an event's occurrence then you are living in a place of denial, which is very dangerous. Denial is living in a

---

[7] www.wateraid.org/uk/our-history (accessed 18th July 2021).

state of refusal, with no recognition of situations that have occurred. If you live in denial, it is likely you will repeat a mistake on multiple occasions, because there will be no recognition of having done something wrong in the first place.

Imagine if I lived in denial when I name-called and upset the child during their swimming lesson. I would have likely used the terrible name-calling technique on other children as well. There would have been many people who would have been hurt by me, instead of just one. The destruction I could have caused would have been endless.

So instead of living in denial, the first step we must take in responding to a mistake is to accept it happened and that we ourselves were at fault. Notice here that I didn't say 'beat ourselves up'. Too many people have a tendency to make a mistake and self-destruct on the inside as a result. This is not a healthy way to go. Conversely, learning to respond with acceptance is the starting point to turning a mistake into a positive and growth-filled experience. Because once you have accepted something, you can then reflect upon it.

2. Reflect

Reflection is the process of analysing experiences with the goal of improving self-performance or how something is done – simply put, *reflection is a doorway to a better version of yourself.* Personally, I think reflection is a crucial tool in any leader's toolkit; after all, who wouldn't want to continually improve? Sadly, though, the current fast pace of the world does not leave much space for reflection, despite the positive impact it can have. Therefore, it is important to make space for refection; *if you try to find space, it won't be there; space has to be made.*

When it comes to responding to mistakes, this space to reflect is essential. Only in this space can you truly analyse what happened. It will tell you what went wrong while also helping you to identify how things could have gone differently if you had acted in another way. Thinking back to my swimming teaching, I could analyse that name-calling was not a positive way of trying to motivate someone to swim. I could then question and look into other approaches of communication that I might use, which may have a better impact in similar situations in the future.

As you do this, you are constantly bettering yourself and those who you lead and influence; or, in other words, when you 'as the leader get better, everyone gets better'.[8] It is only through a process of reflection that lessons are learned to make this possible. Don't underestimate what making time to reflect could do for you and how it can take your leadership to the next level.

3. Implement

Having accepted you made a mistake and taken the time to reflect on how you could have handled the situation better, you are now ready to implement your new strategies, ideas, methods and behaviours. Implementing

---

[8] Quote used weekly on the Craig Groeschel Leadership Podcast, www.youtube.com/watch?v=UI7NOtRmWNc&list=PLfd9RiSXWAX6 3y6ZXYrBtyN05jy3BGEPg&index=42 (accessed 9th August 2022).

something new and improved is the key moment that declares to the world that you have learned from your mistake. It shows your mistake has not defined you, but rather you have used it to become a better version of yourself and a better leader.

When I reflected on the situation with the child at swimming, one of the things I realised was that I didn't know anything about them other than their name. So I decided I would ask some questions to find out what they liked. As I did this, I noticed something special begin to happen. They started to smile. Not only that, they were laughing as we talked. They were enjoying themself, and also began to improve at their swimming.

If you take time to accept your mistakes, reflect on them and implement new strategies, you will see improvements in yourself and those you influence, just like I did with this child.

Summary: *Your mistakes don't have to define you. When you make a mistake, accept it happened, reflect upon it and implement something new.*

7
Working on Your Weakness

For when I am weak, then I am strong.
(2 Corinthians 12:10)

Just as mistakes are normal in life, so too is the fact that we all have weaknesses. No one is perfect – and that's OK! If we all had the same strengths and weaknesses, life would be pretty boring. Although weaknesses are normal, it is good practice to be able to identify and be aware of them. This is really important for leaders, because *being in leadership will always put you in a position where your weaknesses are exposed.*

While some weaknesses are not harmful, there are others that could have a real negative effect on those you are trying to lead – I learned this the hard way in a fateful English class… You see, as I was growing up, my biggest weakness by far was the issue of anger. I had a very short fuse. I became frustrated and wound up easily, which often led me to shout and show my frustration in some way – hitting walls was a personal favourite.

I did my best to contain this anger issue to places where I could get away with it. Mainly, it would happen at home, as I was always too well behaved in school – the fear of being told off by a teacher often outweighed any level of anger and frustration I may have felt – I'm sure my Mum wished I thought the same at home too. However, the writing was on the wall one fateful English class, when everything went wrong.

My teacher had instructed the class to copy down what was written on the board, although this was a problem for me as one of the other boys in the class had stolen my pen. As he walked around the classroom, my teacher could see that I wasn't writing anything down. He simply asked, 'Andy, why are you not writing anything down?'

This was a very appropriate thing for him to ask; after all, I wasn't writing anything down! However, I lost it… 'How do you expect me to write anything down when someone has stolen my pen?' I roared at him.

From his expression I could see that he was shocked. You could see the thoughts running through his brain: 'This is well-behaved Andy; he doesn't shout at teachers.'

As I could see these thoughts written all over his face, I knew I was in trouble and a big consequence was on the way. I remember thinking about how well I had done to hide my anger in school for so long. But weaknesses will always work their way up to the surface, and the final straw that causes them to break through can often be surprising. Nevertheless, it will happen. No one can hide something forever.

Needless to say, weaknesses being exposed in such a dramatic and potentially harmful way don't cohere to the positive influence that we are trying to achieve on others. Therefore, it is important that we can identify our weaknesses to reduce the potential for negative influence and to maintain our positive influence on those around us.

After my outburst in English, I was asked to stand outside the class and my mum was called by my head of year. However, while it wasn't a nice feeling to have my head of year calling my mum, the conversation that occurred did present me with the opportunity to see someone to help me with my anger. Basically, I was given the chance to go for anger management (it was called something fancier but I knew what I was there for – to deal with my anger).

Anger management, although it sounds like a huge deal, was actually one of the best things I have ever done. It truly changed my life. There were three key steps that I learned when it comes to working on your weakness.

1. Ask: for help

When I attended anger management, I met Sally.[9] You can learn a lot about someone from their posture. Sally's posture was very upright in the chair, her face was always looking at me, engaged with what I was saying, and her smile was gentle and comforting. Everything about Sally's posture made me feel at ease straight away and I could tell that she actually cared about me.

Sally was a wonderful woman. Very early on in our sessions it became clear that the time I was spending with her was of great benefit to me. The impact was so positive I didn't want the allotted number of sessions to end. As a

---

[9] Some names have been changed for anonymity.

result, I asked Sally if I could extend the number of sessions I was allowed, twice!

You may have heard it said many times that *asking for help is not a sign of weakness, but a sign of strength*. But even if you have heard it said many times, please do not take it lightly. I wholeheartedly believe this statement to be true. Had I not asked Sally for those extra sessions, I am not sure I would have received the fullness of help I needed to be able to deal with my anger.

There have been many other moments in life and leadership where I have needed the help and guidance of others in my times of weakness. At each of these junctures I am glad that I was strong enough to ask for help, because it really did have a positive influence on me, which created a domino effect of positive influence on those around me.

Please don't be afraid to ask for help; it could make a huge difference to your life and your leadership – 'even a counsellor needs a counsellor'.[10] Regardless as to where you find yourself on the leadership journey, it is never a bad time to learn that it is OK to ask for help.

2. Attack: the root cause

There are different types of weakness, which are the result of a variety of causes. For example, I have a weakness at horse riding. How do I know this? Well, because I rode a horse once, fell off and have never got back on again. Therefore, I am not good at horse riding because I have not had the right exposure and training in that area. On other occasions, the weakness can simply be because we

[10] Shout out to my friend Joel Arumadri for this quote.

actually aren't gifted at something. Art would be my prime example of this. I did art at school, but was I any good at it? Absolutely not! It just was not my thing.

However, there are the more serious weaknesses, which often have deep roots of causality to them. My anger had multiple factors at its root cause. First of all, I was ratty because I wasn't sleeping very well at the time of my outburst in English, as I had recently suffered a pretty bad jaw injury.

However, there were even deeper roots than this. These roots were the result of childhood trauma and pain that I had never dealt with. There wasn't really anyone I could speak to about these situations growing up, so I bottled everything up – mainly there was no one to talk to because I never asked anyone for help; again, don't ever be afraid to ask for help, because it could be a game-changer for you.

Bottling things up never works. Yet we live in a world where many young people bottle things up and don't talk to anyone about them. This is a big problem, for many reasons. One is the inevitable moment when what is bottled up begins to bubble, and gets to the eventual point where the bottle can no longer contain it. How the contents come out of the bottle, though, will be different for everyone: for me, of course, it was anger.

The beauty of talking to someone about the contents of the bottle (those areas of painful experience) is that it creates a space to attack the root, or the cause, of the issue. When I had my sessions with Sally, it was clear that my anger was caused by a lack of sleep and the pain of my childhood. Therefore, all of the activities Sally went through with me were to address both of these aspects. In doing so, I was a changed teenager.

3. Activate: a new way of living

Those sessions with Sally really did turn things around for me and my anger. At the time of writing this book, it has been fourteen years since that day in the English class and I can honestly say that I have never 'lost it' since – other than the occasional bit of frustration on the golf course. Through asking for help and attacking the root of the issue I was able to activate a new way of living.

The Bible verse we read above shows how God can turn our weakness into strength. Through my sessions with Sally my weakness was turned to strength. The angry teenager that went in did not come out the same. Now I am someone who by nature is very calm; in fact, when I tell people of my past anger issues, they usually do not believe me.

Whatever your weakness, God can turn it into strength. Once that exchange has taken place, there is a freedom for you to walk in. Freedom is an attractive quality. It is something so many people are looking for, especially if they are bottling things up.

This is why it is important for you, as a leader, to work on your weakness. Only leaders who have gone through this process to freedom themselves can lead others to that same place of freedom, as you can only lead others where you have been yourself.[11] This is why it is so valuable to

[11] Ruth Haley Barton, *Strengthening the Soul of Your Leadership* (Westmont, IL: InterVarsity Press, 2018), p 87.

learn how to work on your weakness – learning to lead yourself helps you to best lead others and have an all-round positive influence.

One final point... About ten years after my sessions with Sally, I saw her again. I was speaking at the front of a full church when I noticed Sally in the congregation, watching. After speaking, I was able to go and have a good talk with her. I was really encouraged, as she said she could see how much I had changed and grown, while also commenting on the fact that she had learned from what I said in my talk.

This is another beauty of leadership and influence: the *influenced* in one season can be the *influencer* in another season. Sally greatly influenced my life as a teenager and years later I was able to influence her life. This is what can happen when weakness is turned to strength.

Summary: We all have areas of weakness, some of which can be more harmful on our leadership than others. We should never be afraid to talk to someone about our weakness, because doing so could help identify the root cause of the issue and help activate something new within us. A leader who has been through this process is in the prime position to lead others into freedom too.

8
Do Something Different

Difference can be significant.

Having had my life turned around through my time with Sally, I was living with a completely revamped mindset. I was living with confidence and a new-found level of positivity. The old angry and negative Andy was gone; as described in 2 Corinthians 5:17: 'if anyone is in Christ, he is a new creation; the old has gone, the new has come' (NIV 1984).

With this new-found confidence, I was able to take up many opportunities to be a positive influencer. Some of these, though, were not exactly the types of opportunities I would usually have gone for. They were different. They were new experiences. Some may say they were somewhat out of my comfort zone.

This is precisely what happened as I entered into my second year of sixth form. Each year those students going into their final year were able to put themselves forward to be head boy or girl. Naturally there was a process to go through, which everyone knew was finalised by a speech given to the whole of the sixth form and their teachers and the school. It was a daunting process, to say the least.

I decided to put myself forward.

Four other boys also put themselves forward, and in all honesty, I was the wild card of the five. All of the others were either very popular or very clever. They were the types of people you would expect to be head boy – and rightly so! I looked up to them. Their personalities, temperaments and skills certainly hit all the leadership criteria for the role.

These boys were so great, they had it all – the gifting and the popularity. I couldn't help but ask myself the same question over and over again: 'How do I stand a chance against them?' To be honest, I think everyone had that same question going through their minds about me. In fact, I'm sure many students and teachers alike wondered why I had even put myself forward.

I was expected to come last.

As the expectation on me was so low, I knew that I had nothing to lose. Furthermore, I was fully aware that my speech was going to have to be something pretty special if I was going to have any chance. I needed to stand out from the rest. So, with some ideas from my mum, I decided do something different.

Things that are different are often memorable. Admittedly, different can be either good or bad. However, doing something different from everyone else works tremendously well when you are trying to stand out from the crowd and make an impression. That is exactly what happened for me.

I was very taken aback by the positive response my speech received. People loved it! Many people said how they thought it was funny, many described how unexpected they felt it was, and others said they were surprised by the boldness I showed to do what I did. Doing something different seemed to connect with people really well. In fact, the response was so good that, against all the odds, I was voted in as deputy head boy. Amazing!

This was a big lesson in leadership for me. Here are some points for you to consider when doing something different, along with how these points tied in to my head boy application speech.

1. Do something different, not something conforming

OK, so I am sure you are wondering what the 'something different' was that I did in the speech. Well, I did what is called a 'wake-up, shake-up'. This is basically doing some dance-based actions and getting others to follow you – a bit like a warm-up in an upbeat gym class. So whereas all the other boys were speaking for their whole speech, my plan was clearly something different. I got everyone who was watching the speech to stand up, and asked them all to follow along with the actions – which they did.

I wanted to do something different for my speech, with the aim of standing out. However, there are many occasions where we find ourselves just wanting to fit in. In many ways this can be the easy option. Although, just because something is easier doesn't necessarily mean that it's better.

One of the huge issues with trying to fit in is the likelihood of losing yourself in the process – the idea that you will change who you are and what you do in order to be accepted by others. However, it is never a good idea to do something where you lose yourself. Therefore, in doing something different, it is important to do something that is still very much *you*. I love physical exercise, so leading something similar to a gym class warm-up in my speech was very much *me*.

There are times when the easiest way to be different is also the simplest. Be yourself. Whatever your ways of being different are, own them! *If you can embrace who you are it is more likely you will have the confidence to do something different.* Why conform to the patterns of the world[12] when you were born to be different?

2. Do something different, not something stupid

While at face value it could seem as though my 'wake-up, shake-up' was a crazy idea, there was a method behind it – a method in the madness, as they say. After completing the 'wake-up, shake-up', I explained how people will want to put someone in leadership that they are willing to follow. Furthermore, I emphasised how I thought I could lead them all well, as they had followed me during the speech. From comments afterwards I was pleased to hear that this had been understood.

Having an appropriate method is very important when it comes to doing something different. Without a clear method and thought-through rationale to back it up, doing something different can in fact look very strange to those looking on.

---

[12] See Romans 12:2.

So when you fancy having a go at doing something different, don't forget to think and use your brain. Plan properly, understand why you are doing what you are doing and help others to see clarity in your rationale. Be sensible, not stupid.

3. Do something different, not something too risky

The same applies when it comes to taking risks. *There is a big difference between risk and stupidity.* Risk is thought out, with an acknowledgement of the various possible outcomes. Stupidity is jumping into a swimming pool head first without checking how deep the water is – it hurts!

In my head boy speech, one of my other ploys to be different was to do my speech without the use of notes. Where everyone else stood behind the lectern with their paper notes and spoke out their thoughts, I took no notes with me and held the microphone to allow me the freedom to walk around.

Of course, taking no notes up was risky, because at any point I could have lost where I was up to and forgotten what to say – which would have been very embarrassing. However, I practised my speech a number of times with my mum, which allowed me to get my speech into my system. I knew the speech like the back of my hand. It was familiar to me.

So while there was a risk present, the risk was considerably reduced because I had used my preparation time effectively. Good preparation will always help you to take risks as you step out and do something different.

***Summary:** Doing something different has the potential to engage with people in a very powerful and memorable way. We are all made differently, meaning we can all do the same task, but do it in a multitude of ways. To have a positive influence in our leadership we must learn to do things without conforming to the patterns of the world and by taking appropriate risks along the way.*

9

Unseen Results

Faithfulness produces results, though they are not always seen.

After being voted deputy head boy, I was determined to use the position of leadership for positive influence. As I prayed to God about how this could look, God placed in my heart the vision to start a new group in the sixth form. This group was called BIG club (Believe in God club), a group designed to help people explore the Christian faith and to experience the love that Jesus has for them.

BIG club met every Wednesday and ran throughout the entirety of the academic year. Each session discussed a key topic that was pressing on people's minds at the time, which seemed to engage all those who attended.

One of the biggest challenges any leader faces is how to measure and know whether what they have done has been successful or not. The main reason for this difficulty is that feedback is not always given. This can make it hard to distinguish if people have really grasped what you were trying to achieve.

In the world of physics, one of Newton's laws describes how action and reaction go hand in hand with each other. When one thing happens, a natural response occurs as a result. Yet in leadership this does not always appear to be the case, especially if you are not receiving feedback from others on what you are doing, or if you aren't seeing your desired results.

I certainly found this when leading BIG club, particularly when we were given the opportunity to deliver an assembly to the whole of the sixth form.

The head of sixth form was a very generous lady, and she loved giving a voice to students – she was a real *elevator* who gave students a platform. When I asked her if it would be possible for BIG club to lead an assembly, she was more than happy to open that door for us.

As the day came around for us to lead the assembly, I had many thoughts and emotions going through my mind. First, I was really excited. This was such a brilliant opportunity to share about the love of Jesus with the 250 people in the sixth form. It was a moment that I knew would never be available again, so I was pumped and ready to share.

However, I was also pretty nervous. Other than my crazy head-boy speech, I had never spoken in public before. Not to mention that I'd be sharing in front of all my friends and peers. 'Who knows what they might think about me after this?' was a constant thought.

Thankfully, those nervous feelings did not last. In fact, as I got up to speak, I wasn't nervous at all – we can thank God for that one! I felt like the assembly went well. From people's facial expressions it appeared as though they were listening intently; they even laughed at the funny bits!

However, as the rest of the day went by, I became increasingly aware that I had no idea if what I'd said in the assembly had had any impact on anyone. Many people came up to me afterwards with nice comments, like how they'd enjoyed it or that they thought everything was well presented.

While those comments were encouraging, they weren't fully what I wanted to hear. They weren't the results I desired. I was so desperate for someone to be impacted in a powerful way by what they had heard. But, at the time, it didn't seem like anyone was...

Unfortunately, you will soon find that there are often more unseen results than visible results in leadership. But just because you can't see any results, it does not mean nothing is happening. For starters, *God is often working in ways we cannot see.* So while we can't see what is going on inside the hearts and minds of others, God can. This means we need to trust God as we lead and do all He has called us to do.

Having said that, though, this does not necessarily stop our human desires, which like the idea of seeing results for our investments. So the question then arises: how do we keep going, if we aren't seeing the results?

When results are not being seen, there is a call for us as leaders to remain faithful to the cause. There is something special about being invested for the long haul. There is a fruitfulness that comes with not giving up. If you are going to make it in leadership and continue to work towards positive influence, one of the greatest lessons to learn is the lesson of remaining faithful.

Here are some things you can do to help you keep going and remain faithful, even when results are unseen.

1. Remind yourself why you are doing what you are doing

I started BIG club because I wanted people to understand the love of Jesus for themselves. Anyone who starts any project will usually have a reason, or a *'just cause'*, as to why they want to do it. Holding tight to your *'just cause'* is one of the best tools that will help you stay in the game for the long haul.[13]

This is because the *'just cause'* helps to create vision and acts as a springboard for new ideas. It also allows you to keep your core beliefs at the centre of all that you do. This means you won't be prone to losing yourself, team members or the vision along the way.

The *'just cause'* gives you something to fight for. It is what gives you the energy when results are not coming, because you have a vision of what could be in the future. When the BIG club assembly didn't seem to have impacted anyone on a deep level, it would have been easy to have given it all up.

However, that is not what we decided to do. We kept going, because of our *'just cause'*. By keeping going and continuing to put BIG club sessions on weekly, as we already were doing, a space was created for people to come and hear about Jesus.

Which is what happened. As the year passed, more and more people started to attend the group. Our first session

---

[13] Simon Sinek, *The Infinite Game* (New York: Penguin, 2020), p 34.

only had ten people in attendance, but by the end of the academic year, we had fifty-two members. If we had forgotten our *'just cause'* the growth would never have happened. The *'just cause'* gave us the strength to endure.

Whether you are leading a group, or whether you are giving your friend advice for the thousandth time, remember why you are doing it and that will empower you to carry on.

2. *Remind yourself that it is normal for things to be unseen*

It can be easy to say, 'Remind yourself why you are doing what you are doing,' but we must also not forget the simplest of truths in doing so. It is a fact that not everything in life is seen. For example, we don't see our heart pumping blood around our body, yet we understand and believe that a result is taking place, despite being unable to see it with our own eyes.

There are often amazing things going on in unseen places. We need to remember that this is a normal part of life. In doing so, we will take the pressure off ourselves. There are too many occasions, particularly as young people, where people put shed-loads of weight on themselves to hit big milestones. While it's good to aim high, it's not good to overwhelm yourself in the process.

There are a number of reasons why people put this pressure on themselves, such as feeling insecure and needing results to validate themselves, or finding it tough to relinquish control. If you stick by the advice to simply control what you can control, you will also control the amount of pressure you put yourself under, and you will also be able to feel at peace that results are happening, even if they are in unseen places – because God is always working.

3. Remind yourself to celebrate your wins

Over the years, I have heard success defined in many different ways. Most people see success as reaching the end goal or achieving certain targets. However, seeing success like this can, at times, leave you with a lack of joy in your life, because you become consumed with targets.

Personally, I don't know anyone who wants to live their life without any joy – I know I certainly don't. Therefore, if we are going to maintain the joy in our life, we may need to redefine what we see as success.

Like most people, I love a good reason to have a celebration. Celebrating is good for us, and it definitely helps bring some joy into our lives. This is why we need to bring celebration into our leadership and why we need to take time to celebrate our wins.

Success is not just the end goal; success is every step along the way. Every step is a win that can be celebrated. Celebrate progress. Celebrate how far you have come. Celebrate when things have improved. This will bring so much more joy into your leadership, and it will help you to keep working towards the *'just cause'*.

At BIG club, we used to celebrate every time we got a new member of the group. When a new person came into the room for the first time, everyone stood up and gave that person a resounding round of applause. The atmosphere and joy in the room was electric. It's worth finding reasons to celebrate, because every person and every bit of growth is worth celebrating.

About three years after the BIG club assembly, I was out having some food with my friends, when we happened to see another girl who had been in the sixth form with us. Having not seen her for a few years, I was keen to see how she was doing, especially as I knew that after sixth form she had spent some time working with an organisation in Asia helping to serve those in need.

Her stories of her time in Asia were amazing. Obviously, she had been a blessing to many people out there. I was incredibly inspired by all she had done. As I asked more and more about her time in Asia, I came to ask the question, 'What was it that made you want to go out there and serve the poor?'

Her response surprised me.

'Well, do you remember that assembly you did in sixth form?' she asked. 'It all started there. As you spoke, I felt like there was something in me, telling me that I needed to go to Asia and help people.' I couldn't believe it. She continued, 'Then, as I was away, I saw the people living with the faith in Jesus that you spoke about in the assembly. It opened my eyes and I now have this new faith in my life.'

Needless to say, I was delighted with this story. For three years I had thought that the BIG club assembly had had no impact whatsoever. Apparently, I was wrong.

This is why we need to remain faithful in our leadership – because even though it may not always seem as though we are getting the results we want, we never know what God may be doing in people in unseen places.

So I want to encourage you as you read this. Keep going. Remain faithful, even if the results are unseen. Because, even if it's for one person out of 250, it's worth it!

Summary: *Some results are visible, but many are not. As leaders we need to learn to remind ourselves why we are doing what we are doing, and remain faithful to the cause, even if the results are unseen. Redefining how we see success and understanding that God is working in ways we cannot see will help us greatly to remain faithful – right to the end.*

10
Listen to the Right Voices

You can't choose who's around you, but you can choose who you are around.

One of the most significant lessons for any leader to learn is the ability to discern which are the right voices to listen to. This was a lesson I needed to learn fast in my own leadership journey. Even in the early days, I realised how opinionated people are. Regardless as to how you are doing in leadership, or how big your influence is, people will always talk.

Some of what people say can be extremely encouraging, which will naturally give you energy to keep going. However, there will be many times when the words people choose to say about you may be very negative. There are even seasons where it feels like almost everyone is against you. Personally, I have faced a number of seasons where this has been the case. To be honest, these times are not pleasant. It can leave you feeling alone, isolated, and can even take you to the extreme levels where you may even consider giving up.

Sadly, young people are often left feeling these negative emotions, that they don't have a voice and aren't listened to – even if what they are saying is *right*. If you feel like this, then please be encouraged – you are exactly who I wrote this book for. I understand these feelings, having experienced them myself many times.

Having said that, though, this is exactly why it is vital that you choose to listen to the right voices, as the voices you listen to will always have a big impact on you. *Your progress in leadership will depend on the voices you listen to.* Like I said earlier, people will either be an *influencer* or an *influenza* on your life – they will either make you better or make you sick.

Obviously, we want to be surrounded by those voices that make us better. These voices are the ones that help our influence to grow and give us the strength to be sustained for leadership in the long haul.

These voices come in many different forms. Here are some of the voices you need, how I would define them and how they can play out in our journey of leadership and influence.

1. Coaches

The term 'coach' can be used as an umbrella term to describe voices that may also be called mentors, spiritual directors or counsellors.[14] Basically, a coach is someone who journeys with you as you negotiate your way through life. They will give you encouragement and inspiration

---

[14] See Dave Smith, *God's Plan for your Well-Being* (Surrey: CWR, 2020), p 130.

when you need it, while also challenging you to reflect and see things from a different viewpoint or perspective. As a result, it is often most appropriate and beneficial to have a coach who is older and more experienced than yourself.

Throughout my life I have had different coaches at different times, based upon where I was geographically located and the type of work I was doing – you need a coach who is experienced and has influence in the same, or very similar, spheres that you are in yourself.

When I was in the world of swimming, and trained regularly for races, I had a guy called Steve who did lots to help me improve in my leadership. Steve always took time to listen to all my life concerns and always gave a wise, well-reasoned response to my problems. Steve also challenged me in many ways.

One of the key ways Steve challenged me was in the way I saw myself. Growing up, I really didn't value myself at all. Steve was someone who brought a change to this – which was priceless, as it taught me that *you can't truly value others until you truly value yourself.*

2. Comrades

A comrade is someone you journey through life with in close proximity, as you head towards a common purpose. In simple terms, I would say that a comrade combines friendship with purpose. From my own experience, these can be the hardest people to find. Therefore, it may take considerable amounts of prayer and discernment to make sure you have the right comrades in your life. Furthermore, as comrades offer such close proximity in the relationship, you generally don't need many of them.

I would say that I have three comrades in my life: Dave, Nathaniel and Emily. These are my closest friends and help me pursue God's purpose for my life better than anyone. Admittedly, I did have to wait a long time before these people walked into my life, as Dave and Nathaniel only entered it when I was twenty-one and Emily entered when I was twenty-three. I can honestly say that they were worth the wait.

One of the questions you may have is: how do you identify if someone is a comrade or not? For me, I would say that a comrade is someone you have the deepest conversations and largest laughs with, all knitted together. This is what happens every time I am with Dave, Nathaniel and Emily. My stomach is often sore from endless belly laughs and my heart is full from the depths of the conversation.

Every leader needs good comrades in their life. They know you better than anyone, encourage you more than most and make you laugh, even when things get tough – and everyone needs a good laugh, because laughing is healthy.

3. Colleagues

Don't be put off by the word 'colleague' here. This word does not simply relate to those people you work with, but rather it refers to every person you work with as part of a team. Colleagues can very easily be comrades, as the idea of a colleague is someone you work alongside to achieve a particular goal, target or outcome. But in doing so, you will do life with these people. They will be your team. They will be the ones you lean on in the tough times and laugh with in the good. Without the right team/colleagues, tasks would be much harder to achieve. These people/voices are essential.

I have had many of these people/voices in my life at different points of my leadership journey, which you will hear more about later. During my days teaching swimming, though, I had Karen, Richard, Olga, Rachel, Chris, Steven, Catherine, Becky, Rachael, Ruth, Elise, Ali and Ronnie, to name but a few. We really were a great team together, mainly because we were led so brilliantly by the incredible Karen. Karen knew the strengths of each member of the team and played to them. She positioned each of us to teach children at the ability level which we were most comfortable teaching, alongside another teammate who Karen knew we would work well with. As a result, being around the right people helped our team to function in the best way possible. It was Karen's leadership in putting us together that truly made us a dream team.

Every leader needs a dream team around them, so make sure your team or group is made up of the right people. Your influence depends on it.

4. Casuals

Casuals are friends that you have who help you get away from everyday life. Taking time out is essential for every leader, as when you are in leadership, pursuing purpose daily and helping others frequently is a fast track to regularly becoming tired. After all, you are not a superhero; your body has limits and needs re-energising from time to time. The right people in this category of relationship will naturally give your life a sense of refreshment whenever you spend time with them.

I have a number of casuals in my life who allow me to do the things I enjoy and enrich my time with laughter and quality conversations. One of these is Danny. Danny and I will often go to play golf together. I give him a lift to the golf course and in return he makes me a delicious, fully loaded sandwich to have halfway through the round. Then on the way home we stop for a coffee and chat about faith and the blessings of life. Time with Danny always reignites a spark of positivity within me.

Another casual I have is Stew. Stew and I currently live very far away from each other, but that doesn't get in the way of our friendship. Every so often one of us will message the other saying, 'Zoom?' That's it. One word, with the simple underlying message of, 'Let's have a chilled catch-up for an hour.' It's exceptionally casual, particularly when Stew starts talking about his frog and his favourite Christian memes on social media; but nevertheless, time with Stew is very much needed, as it gives me great joy, energy and refreshment.

Make sure you make space for casuals, because everyone needs time to chill.

Summary: *The voices you listen to will have a big impact on you. They will either make you better, or make you sick. In choosing the voices you want around you, make sure you choose the ones that add value to your life and leadership. By learning this lesson now, you are taking huge strides towards the long haul of sustained influence.*

Part summary

This part of the book has focused on 'learning to lead'. And although this may be one of the first sections in the book, that does not mean that you only learn when you are starting out. In fact, learning never stops. There will always be parts of your weakness you can work on; mistakes will still happen and continue to give you a chance to learn. People will always talk and you will constantly have to evaluate the voices you choose to listen to. So, no matter what opportunities come your way, don't forget, that every opportunity is an opportunity to learn.

Part Three
Taking the Lead

The more you learn in leadership, the more likely you are to progress. As this happens, you may be promoted to a specific position or given a title with an emphasis on leadership; or there may naturally be added responsibility that comes your way as a result of your sphere of influence increasing. This section will help you see how your sphere of influence can enlarge and give you some pointers on how to truly embrace the responsibility required to steward all of those you are leading. Now is the time to *take the lead*.

11
Putting Yourself Out There

Champion yourself.

Once my time in the sixth form was complete, I started a degree in sports therapy. It had been my dream for many years to work in professional football, specifically in the medical department of a club. This was a big ambition. After all, I knew I wasn't going to be the only one with this dream. Sport is competitive, even when it comes to trying to work in the medical department!

All of us will face moments like these. Times when you aren't the only one bidding for something – a job, a place in university, tickets for a concert, or even for that must-have product. There can be a feeling of pressure in these moments. It's as if your whole life hangs in the balance.

You are desperate to be the one who gets through, against all the odds – even against those voices that say you'll never make it. But how do you do this? Well, quite simply, you need to stand out from the crowd. But, most importantly, you need to be willing to put yourself out there. You need to be willing to take a risk. Even if you take a risk and it doesn't pay off, there is peace that comes in knowing you gave it your best shot.

I was blessed to live out my dream of working in football. I even saw myself get many promotions. Each new role saw an increase to my influence and responsibility, because at every step, I was climbing up the leadership ladder.

However, none of these steps would have taken place without my willingness to give 100 per cent effort at each stage. You can't be a leader without putting yourself out there. Leadership is not about being passive and waiting for things to happen; rather, *leadership is about being constantly proactive and engaging with the world around you.*

By engaging, you put yourself in a position to stand out and be noticed. This is what I did as I progressed through the world of football. Sometimes it was obvious that what I was doing was being noticed; however, there were some instances where I had no idea that what I was doing was helping me to stand out from the crowd at all.

Anyway, here are some ways in which you can put yourself out there and stand out from the crowd as you look to progress through leadership and increase your influence in the sphere God has placed you in.

1. Use your contacts

Here is a fact: *God is the best contact you have.* God can open doors that nobody else can: 'What he opens no one can shut' (Revelation 3:7). God can make a way, even when it seems impossible.

For me, communication with God is the most important part of leadership, for many reasons. One reason is that He knows where you will be most effective as a leader. Therefore, in prayerfully communicating with Him, you are allowing Him to open the right doors to place you in the sphere where you will have the greatest impact and influence.

A door opening for me to work in football was all down to God's positioning. This particular positioning allowed me to gain a contact called Mitch, whose family went to my uncle's church, which allowed for the initial contact with him. Mitch was a physiotherapist and is one of the nicest, pleasantest and most caring men I have ever met, which made him such a great leader. Furthermore, he was the kind of guy who would do anything he could to help, support and open doors for those he believed in. Thankfully, I was one of these people.

Having met Mitch originally when I was seventeen, a good relationship was formed. A few years later, Mitch happened to move to the football club just down the road from where I was living. I sent him a letter to see if I could volunteer to work for the club as a student. Amazingly, Mitch created space for a door to be opened and, through God's incredible timing and provision, I was living the dream of working in professional football. Not only that, but all of the other opportunities I had while working in football came because of Mitch.

I guess what I'm really saying here is that it really is all about who you know, and if you know God, you have the greatest contact of all.

2. Start small

Dreaming big, I believe, is a good thing. However, in dreaming big, we must be willing to take the right steps before we can get there. Starting small is always the best place to begin. Although it may not always look like what we imagined right away, these small beginnings will lead to greater things in the long run. Whatever you do, 'Do not despise ... small beginnings' (Zechariah 4:10, NLT).

Prior to working at the higher levels of football, I started at the bottom of the pyramid. One of the best attributes someone can have when trying to put themselves out there is experience. *Starting small is the best way to gain experience.* Often the easiest way to get experience is by volunteering in places that are on the lookout for extra help. These opportunities are good, providing there is appropriate oversight by a responsible person for the work you are doing, as this will aid your development. Similarly, using your contacts is good, even in trying to start small.

3. Be honest

Once I had worked in the lower areas of the football pyramid and spent some time gaining work experience with Mitch, I was presented with an opportunity to work for another club. The position I was able to apply for was one that would progress me in my leadership, as it was at a higher level than I had previously held.

Having applied for the job and been for an interview, I was delighted when I got the job. To be honest, I was surprised when I got the call to say that my application had been successful, as I knew that many of the other people who had applied were much more qualified and experienced than myself.

So I decided to ask my new club why they had given me the job. They informed me that during the interview I was the only one who appeared to be honest when answering questions, especially when asked questions I didn't know the answer to. Apparently, others who were interviewed tried to weave eloquent answers together and even tried to fake it, whereas I was upfront and honest to say when I didn't know something.

It was honesty that got me the job, and faking it that prevented the others from getting it. You will never progress in leadership by being fake. Don't ever try to force your progress in leadership. Progress happens best when you are humble enough to be honest.

4. Go above and beyond

From what I observed during my time in football and through other experiences, I have seen that *being hardworking is an essential attribute for being influential.* There is always a choice in leadership: you can do just enough to get by, or you can give it everything you've got and go above and beyond. Going above and beyond really helps you to put yourself out there. Above all, it highlights that you care and that you are prepared to do what it takes to lead and have influence for the long haul.

While I was working at one particular football club, we were particularly understaffed. There were three of us filling at least two or three jobs each and working many more hours than we were contracted to do – please note there are unhealthy elements to this kind of working! However, our teamwork was impeccable and the players on the pitch were doing exceptionally well. *There are more chances for positive results when you invest highly.* Every team needs people who are willing to go above and beyond for the sake of greater influence.

As I continued to work hard as a volunteer and go above and beyond myself, I was offered an employed position within the club. This role was a head of department position – despite only being twenty-one years of age. It meant higher responsibility, and greater opportunities to bring change and influence. Hard work does pay off.

5. Acknowledge your strengths

Here's a question for you: how good are you at telling others what your strengths are? For some of you this may come naturally, but I'm guessing that it is a pretty hard thing for the majority to do; I would say it is also the case for me. If you ask me to tell you my weaknesses, I could sit you down with a nice cup of tea and some biscuits for hours to tell you about them. As for strengths? Well, that would not be so straightforward.

When I finished my last job in football, my boss sat me down to review how he thought I had performed in the job. This identified what I had done well alongside giving me some pointers as to how I could improve my leadership in the future. The main aspect my boss told me I needed to improve was the ability to share my strengths with others. He told me that if I could master this, my influence would improve even further, because sharing my strengths would create further opportunities.

You have strengths; don't hide them. After all, your strengths are all God-given. So sharing them will give Him glory and increase the influence you can have.

Summary: *Putting yourself out there is not about showing off, but about helping you to progress. This allows you to take the lead at higher levels, increasing your responsibility, while growing your influence. So use your contacts, take small steps, be honest with everyone, work hard and know that it is OK to champion yourself and share the strengths that God has placed inside you.*

12
Leaving an Effective Legacy

*People will remember you more for the atmosphere
you create than the results you make.*

My time working in football was amazing, but, like most things in life, it did not last forever. I knew God was calling me to something different and was taking me into a new season. Moments like these can leave you with mixed feelings. There is the excitement of what is to come, but there is also the sadness of what will be left behind. This was exactly how I felt leaving football.

I was excited, because I was heading back to university to study a Master's degree in physiotherapy. I was looking forward to what I would learn in my lectures; the idea of growing and becoming better has always been something I've liked. However, what excited me the most was the idea of meeting new people. Doing the Masters meant leaving home to live with people I'd never met and also meant I'd have to find a new church. Lots of change, but many opportunities to make new acquaintances.

Despite meeting lots of new people, I was somewhat surprised by how much I was hearing from the *old* people.

Months after I had left my last position in football, working in the lead role for all things medical and fitness in a professional team's academy, I was still getting messages and phone calls from the youth team players and other staff members asking for my help and support. It seemed that after I'd left, things took a turn for the worse within the team.

Prior to my moving on, the academy team was excelling in the league and all was going well. Then after I had gone, the team lost a string of matches back to back. The morale in the camp was all over the place and no one seemed to know what to do – except call *me*. The coach, Nathan, even called and asked if it would be possible for me to travel across to speak to the players in the dressing room before the next match. So I did, and they happened to win.

After that, things seemed to stabilise within the team. The atmosphere in the dressing room was better and performance levels seemed to improve again… although I was still getting messages from players wanting someone to talk to and help them out.

One year later, I went to see the team again, as they were playing not too far away from my university. As I arrived, I looked out onto the pitch to see them warming up, under the brightness of the floodlights. They were doing their usual warm-up routine, but from what I could see, the person leading the warm-up was not someone I recognised. As I looked around more, the brightness of the floodlights brought to my attention six other figures I did not recognise.

Finally, I saw someone I did know: Nathan. Nathan was the coach of the youth team. When I worked for the club, Nathan and I operated incredibly well together. He did all the coaching parts and I did all the medical and fitness aspects. Nathan and I knew how to get the best out of one another and the players. We understood our roles and we understood how our different skills worked together for the team on the whole. We led each other and everyone else.

Seeing him again was excellent, but as I spoke to him, there was one key question running round my mind, which I could not help but ask, 'Nathan, who are all these new people? I don't know any of them.'

He responded, 'They are the people we have had to bring in to replace you.'

Now, before you think I'm awesome, please note that I wasn't actually qualified enough to do the leadership role that I had been given in the first place, which is exactly why I had gone back to university. If I hadn't gone back to study, I would have lost my job anyway, because certain guidelines and legislation meant that someone with better qualifications was required to fill the leadership position I was occupying. Nevertheless, I was pretty amazed that they needed seven people to replace me.

Things got even crazier a few months later, as I attended the wedding of Joey, one of the other team coaches. Nathan was able to introduce me to all the new staff members that I had seen that night under the floodlights. Strangely, though, all of the people Nathan introduced me to already knew who I was. Furthermore, most of them were asking when I was coming back, because they needed me.

These were people who had vastly more experience than I did and they were much more qualified. So why would they ask me to come back? Because I had left a legacy.

There are many ways to leave a legacy. The most obvious are those that are performance-based, like when someone wins gold medals in the Olympics or achieves greatness in business or by fighting for justice. However, the most common legacies are not always the ones that happen on *purpose* but the ones that happen organically.

People will remember you more for the atmosphere you create than the results you make.

This is what I realised from all that happened after I left football. Leaving a legacy has nothing to do with your qualifications or age – I wasn't fully qualified to do my role in football and was still very young. *The greatest legacy you leave will always be based around how you make people feel.*

There is nothing to stop you from doing this now. To help you along the way, here are two things you must do and think about as you take the lead, in order to leave an effective legacy.

1. Consistency

The first component that helps in leaving a legacy is consistency. Consistency does not just refer to one particular area, but all of them. This includes things like showing up on time, always being present and engaging in conversation, giving maximal effort to all tasks, having a positive mindset and attitude, and treating everyone equally and with value. I tried my best to do all of these things while in football.

You may look at this short list and think that it should be a given for everyone in leadership to do all of these things, but you would be surprised by how many don't. The fact is, those you are leading will always pick up on stuff – whether that is you being late or you having a negative attitude, they will notice it.

As a leader, one of the main reasons we want to be consistent is to help create an atmosphere where relationships can form and be nurtured. *Consistency helps relationships to grow.* People like knowing what to expect from their leaders – and consistency helps this to become a reality. When this consistency is positive consistency, the atmosphere established is one of safety, care and value.

I totally believe this is what happened with regard to my relationship with the players I was leading in football. Those feelings of safety, care and value were all well formed during my days working with them week in, week out. As a result, when they desired help and positive encouragement, I was the person they came to, both when I worked for the team and even after I had left.

As those players continued to ring me in the years after my departure, I realised how much people want leaders who make them feel valued. The problem, though, is that if people are only valued *some* of the time, they end up feeling of no value at all. *People need consistency to feel valued.*

I believe this is one of the most significant elements of God's character for us; the Bible says how He is the 'same yesterday and today and for ever' (Hebrews 13:8) – you can't get any more consistent than that! Just as God is consistent in His goodness to us, we too should be consistent with those we lead, to help them feel valued for who they are.

2. *Authenticity*

If anyone is in leadership, they are usually someone who is highly motivated, with aims of seeing progression in their particular sphere of influence. While progress and growth are good things, the question of motivation is something that should be asked.

Sadly, there are leaders who are only in the game for themselves. The only person they want to see benefit, progress and get all the accolades is them. These leaders see those under their leadership only as a means for their own gain. This is not leadership. This is not real. These leaders are not the real deal. Nobody wants a leader who is not leading with the right motives. Like with consistency, it is easy to spot those with improper motives who lack authenticity.

However, a leader who is authentic will have more suitable motives for being in leadership. They will value others and want to see them reach their full potential, even if that means those they are leading reach *higher* levels than the leader themself. Authentic leaders care deeply about all those they are influencing and want the best for everyone.

Another part of being authentic is being able to fully be yourself, quirks and all. While in football, I used to message the injured players every evening, so they knew what to expect the next day. First, these messages came via a group message with a silly group name, then there would be some comedy gold (or attempted comedy) in the body of the message, before finishing with an elaborate hashtag to conclude the message.

When the players came in for treatment the next day, there were often great amounts of laughter bouncing around the room as we discussed the previous evening's puns. Then, as the players left the treatment room to head into the gym, they would shout back to me with the hashtag from the message the night before.

These messages were simple and a little bit silly, but what I could see these young players appreciated most was that they got to see the real Andy. I wasn't trying to put a mask on and I wasn't trying to fake it or be someone I wasn't. I was just myself. And, to be honest, when I first started doing the messages, I didn't know or expect them to be such a hit with the players. But that is the beauty of authenticity – sometimes things just work when you are able to be yourself.

As you take the lead, I truly encourage you to be yourself. In doing so, the relationships you build with others will be so much better, and go much deeper, as a result. Don't try to fit in or behave in the way you think everyone expects you to. Be authentically you.

Summary: In order to lead in a way that will leave an effective legacy you need to be consistent and authentic – work hard, value others and be yourself. That's how you create an atmosphere for people to remember.

13
Bossing Time Management[15]

Make time your friend.

The management of time is probably one of the most spoken about topics, yet one of the hardest skills to master within leadership. When you take the lead in any sphere of influence, you automatically become someone whose time is wanted by others. Furthermore, when you take the lead, you also become someone who is in the spotlight, and if you aren't in the spotlight, people will often wonder where you are and ask you to return to a place where they can see you.

As there is such a high demand placed upon those in leadership, one of the biggest battles a leader will face is managing their time. This is especially the case when it comes to unforeseen circumstances. There will always be a variety of troubling situations that arise in life, which will leave people with a desire for a leader's attention and support. Not to mention all of the other activities which will naturally fill the diary.

---

[15] To my friend Anna Briggs – thank you for our conversations that brought this chapter to life!

Before too long, it can be possible for the diary to be so full that a leader can be left feeling lifeless, overwhelmed and burnt out. Hence the need for good time management. Good time management allows a leader the space for life, to experience joy and gain rest, while being productive in their areas of influence. *The greater a leader's management of time, the greater their quality of life.*

After my time in football was over, I returned to university for further study. Studying hard at university teaches you a lot about time management, because you have regular deadlines. What's more, how fast these deadlines come! As soon as one assignment deadline is met, there is another one just around the corner.

For some people, those managing time well, this won't be so much of a problem. However, there are those who don't like to get started right until the last minute, meaning they have to rush and lose a lot of sleep in order to meet some of their deadlines. From my university experience, I would say there are more people who have to pull an all-nighter at some point compared with those who don't.

Personally, throughout all my university studies, one of my aims was to never be in a situation where I needed to pull an all-nighter or have to ask for an extension on an assignment. I was determined to manage my time well, to the degree that I was able to hand in my assignments at least a week prior to the deadline. As I write this, I have thus far completed six years of university study, having met all my time-related goals.

I know some of you will be wondering how this is possible. Well, let me share some key points with you, which I hope will show you that it is much easier to manage time well than you think.

1. Manage the pressure

There will always be pressure to meet deadlines and hit targets while in leadership. Deadlines automatically add pressure. The question is, though, where do you want the pressure to be on your timeline? Because how you manage your time will determine how much pressure you place on yourself.

Let me explain. I'm sure most people have had someone tell them 'not to leave it to the last minute' at some point in their lives. The main reason people say this is to help you try as far as possible to avoid the added stress that a deadline brings. There will always be pressure to complete a task or assignment, whether you like it or not. However, the pressure to complete a task is always less at its beginning. Starting early removes a lot of the stress you will face if you leave everything close to the deadline.

Now, I know that for some people it is all well and good saying this in principle, but in reality you won't be the sort of person who starts early, because you actually need to feel the pressure a deadline creates to get something done. In other words, you use the pressure to your advantage, as you wouldn't get the task done without it.

OK, so using pressure to your advantage can be a good thing. So what I would say is: create your own pressure by making your own deadline. When I was in university, I never worked off the university's calendar; I worked to my own calendar. I gave myself deadlines. This allowed me to use pressure to my advantage and even create space for me to rest, while all the late starters were doing the all-nighters in the library to get assignments finished by the deadline.

The way I look at this is a bit like cooking meat – I apologise to all the vegetarians for this illustration. Fact is: *you can't cook meat without turning up the heat.* It is the heat that allows it to be cooked; in the same way, creating your own deadline produces pressure for you to complete tasks or assignments. Furthermore, when cooking meat, like steak, there are moments when you need to take the meat out of the heat to turn it over. This is also what using your own deadlines can do. By applying pressure early, you create extra space for rest, which is also something to prioritise when managing time effectively.

2. Prioritise rest

Rest is probably one of the most misunderstood aspects of time management, especially in the Western world. As the majority of the West is consumed by productivity, the principle of rest can sometimes be neglected. Neglecting rest can potentially be dangerous and should be avoided.

Thinking back to the 'cooking meat' illustration, if you leave meat in the heat of the oven for too long, the meat will get burnt. It won't look nice and it certainly won't taste nice. I believe this is what happens to those in leadership. Without rest, you will suffer from being burnt out and what you do manage to produce will not look good.

What this shows is how rest is important for both looking after yourself and producing your best leadership.

You produce your best from a posture of rest. No one can continue to give out when they are tired and weary. No one can give out when they are empty; you can only give from what you have. And if you have nothing in the tank, then you'll give out nothing. Your production will cease and you will be incapable of your desired influence.

However, by allowing yourself to rest, your energy will be restored and your tank will be filled, meaning you will have something to give to those you are leading, alongside feeling better within yourself. *You will look after yourself by looking after your time.* Prioritising rest is what allows this to happen.

Rest is not just something to plan, but something that must be protected. Plan it in and make sure nothing gets in the way. While studying at university, my time of protected rest was Saturday mornings and evenings. In the mornings, my friends Dave and Nathaniel and I would take it in turns each week to make breakfast for the group. Additionally, another member of the group would lead a Bible study and the final member would pray for us.

Then in the evenings it would be movies accompanied with snacks from the local corner shop. Our snack choices became very repetitive after a while. Dave would choose crisps and dip, Nathaniel would have cookies and milk, and I would have a full box of grapes – although my healthy option soon went out the window when we all got our own ice cream tubs.

Those Saturdays were precious moments that created many memories and helped build enduring friendships. They were times of rest that we all needed. It gave us life and laughter and, to be honest, I think we would have all struggled in university without those times of rest.

So in your leadership, please prioritise rest – you need it!

3. Make time your friend

In those Bible studies Dave, Nathaniel and I used to have, we often spoke a lot about patience. We would ask questions like, 'What does it mean to be truly patient?', 'What does it look like to live in patience?' and 'How can someone *actually be patient*?' Patience seems to be one of those fruits of the Spirit (Galatians 5:22-23, NLT) that is more difficult to get your head around and do, especially as a young person. Hence why we kept coming round to the same questions over and over again.

It wasn't until a few years after those Saturday morning breakfasts that I seemed to get the answer. I was sitting in my room, reading my Bible, when I came across the word 'patience'. I decided to sit for a while. As I sat, I prayed and asked God the question, 'How can someone *actually be patient*?'

I felt God respond, 'Make time your friend.'

As I sat and reflected on this further, I realised how there are so many people who make time their *enemy*. I'm sure you can think of a time when you were excited for a particular date to arrive, whether that be a birthday, Christmas, a holiday, starting university, getting a job, the day you'll meet the person you'll marry; whatever it is, I'm sure there have been times that you have been extremely frustrated by the time gap between where you are now and where you want to be.

It happens all the time, even more so when you are young and looking forward to various points in life. This is also true with progress in leadership and results in leadership. Time is often seen as a barrier, but really, time wants to be your friend.

I realised that time will always tick by, which therefore gives you a choice: will you use the time well? *Time is something you can either use or lose.* When I say 'use' time, I don't simply mean doing more stuff. I mean having quality time, with time. Rest, for example, would be a quality use of time. On the other hand, scrolling for an hour on social media may not be a good use of time.

How this quality use of time looks for me is very simple. I take time at the end of every day to sit, be still, pray and reflect on my day. I take such care of this time that I will even write my reflections in a journal. As I write some simple bullet points about my day, I think about what I'm thankful for, good stories from the day and the lessons I have learned. I want to get the most out of every day.

It's a bit like when you go swimming. After you've been in the pool, your trunks or swimsuit gets wet, sucking in and holding the water, but with all that wetness you don't really want to put your stuff in your bag. Therefore, you might wring out as much of the water as possible before placing your trunks or swimsuit into your bag.

Making time your friend is exactly like this. You try to look at every day and *wring out* every bit of goodness. In doing so, you remain present, focused and filled with gratitude. Your thoughts are not consumed by where you wish you were, but rather they are fixed on where you are.

In your leadership, *make time your friend.* Let it enlarge your perspective to see things in a new way, keeping you focused on the joy of the present and helping you *wring out* the goodness of every day.

Summary: *Time management is one of the greatest skills a leader can have. In managing time effectively, you will be able to take the lead in a way that is productive, while also bringing space into your life for those activities which you love to do and giving you optimal time to rest properly and fruitfully. Take care of your time, because time is your friend.*

14
Understanding the Power of 'No'

'No' is one of the most powerful and misunderstood words in the English language.

Having come out of football and returned to full-time study, there was a significant amount of free time created in my week. This was a big, yet pleasant, change from the business of professional football, as I had more time to invest my energy into other areas of life that captured my heart and attention.

As a result, I decided to invest in serving my church as much as possible – while, of course, managing my time effectively. There were many opportunities to serve and lead in areas I had not previously experienced.

For example, I joined the homeless outreach team. This gave me an understanding and love for people in society that I had ashamedly dismissed in the past. I also got involved with the church crèche. I was no stranger to children's and youth work, but joining the team who entertained the babies and toddlers was something new for me to experience. I was also given opportunities to lead house groups, youth groups and our church football group. I was more experienced in leading within these spheres, but I grew a lot from the variety of areas I was able to serve and lead in.

Despite serving in a lot of areas, one I longed to serve my church in was public speaking. This was a dream I'd had for a number of years, having felt God speak to me about it years earlier at a summer festival. As this dream pressed heavily on my heart, I went to speak to my church leaders about the possibility of speaking at the front of church.

The conversation was very informative, yet also surprising. I was expecting them to be exceptionally excited by the dream I had for my life. I was thinking they would move every mountain under the sun to make my dream a reality. However, that was not the case. They told me that it would be unlikely for my dream to happen in the church anytime soon, because there was a natural process of leadership to go through before being given an opportunity to speak at the front.

To be honest, all I heard them say, was, 'No.' Admittedly, I was somewhat frustrated with the outcome of the conversation – side note, *frustration always follows unmet expectation*. I could not see why they *wouldn't* allow me the chance to take the lead. After all, God had spoken to me and I was already leading in lots of other areas in the life of the church. To me, surely this was the right time for the next step?

Time is an amazing thing, because as I look back on that conversation with my church leaders, I have nothing but the utmost gratitude for what they said to me. 'No' was by far the best response they could have given me at the time.

Years later, when the chance to speak at the front of a church did come along, I was delighted I hadn't been given this particular opportunity years earlier. At the time I had asked for an opportunity to speak at church, I was nowhere near ready for that platform or level of leadership, but I could only see that years later, when I did come to speak for the very first time.

Timing is everything in leadership. *Promotion to levels you are not ready for can kill your leadership.* If my church leaders had let me speak at church when I wanted to, I would not have been mature enough to take on that level of responsibility. I would probably have done a rubbish job, and I'd have been so embarrassed that it's likely I would have never wanted to lead or stand on a stage ever again.

When you take the lead in any area, your maturity must be able to match the responsibility you are given. My maturity was not at the right level when I had asked for an opportunity to speak, but it was when the time did come. This was entirely down to my church leaders. They invested in my leadership. They put on a leadership small group and invited me to it. They helped me take the right steps at the right time to grow and develop as a leader. And, most importantly for this 'Take the Lead' section, they did give me many opportunities to lead – hence why I was involved in all the areas I mentioned earlier.

Having done the leadership small group, they then asked me to lead a small group with them, before releasing me to lead a small group of my own. These steps were crucial to my leadership development and they were the steps I needed to take before speaking on the stage. They increased my maturity to get me ready for the responsibility.

Looking back, I see clearly how my church leaders never actually *said* 'No' to me, although they did indicate that there was a process. They understood that timing is crucial and that taking adequate steps of preparation is essential, which is why a process is needed. Furthermore, there is so much more to leadership than standing on stages.

What they helped me to see is that *you can still be a leader without standing on a stage.* I will always be grateful for the strong leadership that taught me such a significant lesson.

If you are reading this and you feel frustrated by not being given opportunities for leadership promotion, it might simply be that your process needs to be a little bit longer. Yes, that can be and usually is very frustrating. But there is a power in the word 'No' that is often misunderstood, especially by those of us desperate for further leadership opportunities.

'No' is naturally coupled with 'Yes'. As soon as you say 'No' to one thing you automatically say 'Yes' to something else, and vice versa. For example, if you are asked, 'Would you like a tea or coffee?' and you say, 'Tea, please,' you are in fact saying 'Yes' to tea and automatically saying 'No' to coffee – unless you are one of those people who like a strange concoction of both!

When it comes to taking the lead, the same applies. When we are told 'No' in one area, there are many areas where we can say a resounding 'Yes'. So if you are hearing that word 'No', flip it on its head and see what you can say 'Yes' to. These yeses will enable you to mature in the areas you are currently leading, before taking on the responsibility of your God-given dreams or next steps. *Choose to respond to a 'No' with a resounding 'Yes'.* Here are some areas to say 'Yes' to.

1. Say 'Yes' to servant leadership

One of the biggest, yet most important, things leaders often forget or do not appreciate is the idea of servanthood. Too often, there are leaders who think they are *above* certain tasks or jobs. However, this is not what leadership is about. A good leader is one who is willing to serve, regardless of the task.

I was once told a story about a famous leader who founded a large movement of churches. This leader was well known for their excellent leadership and often spoke at conferences on the subject. At one particular conference, the leader decided that they were not going to give a usual conference talk, but were instead going to get the other church leaders in the room to do something practical.

The leader took them down to the toilets, which did not happen to be the cleanest facilities. I am pretty sure these leaders were exceptionally puzzled to find themselves staring at dirty toilets, when they were expecting a well-rounded talk from the stage. I can guarantee that none of them were expecting what came next: the leader asked them to clean the toilets.

Here, the leader was teaching that *you cannot be a leader without being a servant.* No matter where you find yourself in leadership, you should never be too big to do the small things. Leadership, first and foremost, is about serving. Serving is simply about being available and meeting the needs of others through every task that you put your hands to.

While in my season of not speaking on stages, I put my hands to anything and everything I could, even if I had no idea whether I would be good at it or not. Some of it I was better at than expected, while some things I really wasn't very good at. However, *serving is not about capability; it's about availability.* Similarly, the best leaders are often the ones who are most available to people and most willing to get their hands dirty – after all, hands are made for working.

So, regardless as to where you feel you should be in leadership, there are always opportunities to serve. Take this season to say 'Yes' to servant leadership and you will find yourself learning a lot about what it truly means to be a leader.

2. Say 'Yes' to the process

As described, there is always a process to go through in leadership, especially when it comes to progressing to higher levels and positions. However, it is fully up to you whether you use the time effectively or not. You could easily get caught up in feeling rejected and demotivated if you have faced a 'No', but if you give up in the process, you won't mature and you won't be in a position to take on the higher levels when the opportunity arises.

Therefore, wherever you are, positionally and emotionally, immerse yourself in the present. Continue to maximise the investment of where you are and take responsibility for all you have been given to steward. There is a blessing that comes with longevity; even if it seems like the same thing over and over, there will be layers of learning that take place within you as a result.

Being able to stay in something for the long haul is key to success in leadership. But you can't make it in the long haul without being able to persevere, endure and find joy in the everyday. This is what the process does. It teaches you about these key elements which are paramount for a long life in leadership.

Use this season in the process as a foundation, because you can't build anything without firm foundations. People need leaders who have their foundations in order, because solid foundations help people feel safe in whatever they are building. Foundations are the starting point of progress, but foundations don't firm up without the right process.

So get stuck into the process in this season; because *without the process, you won't progress.*

Summary: *It can be frustrating to hear the word 'No' when you long for progression in leadership. However, leadership is not all plain sailing, and 'No' will come up from time to time. When it does, you need to respond well to this by saying 'Yes' to all you are able to say 'Yes' to. Doing so will enable you to take the right steps in the process before taking on the extra responsibility that comes with taking the lead in new ways. Remember, leadership is never about you, but it is always about those you serve. Wherever you are in leadership, always be prepared to get down on your knees and serve in the dirt, because hands were made for working.*

15
Own the Moment

*Every moment can be owned, if you have the
courage to take the lead.*

During my time at university, while I was in the
leadership small group, God spoke to me about going to
Uganda to set up a sports ministry. The process of
preparation for this trip was immense. I was going to
Uganda for seven months; thankfully, I had eighteen
months to plan – although those eighteen months did
coincide with having to finish my degree. Every day
counted to make sure everything was adequately
prepared for before I left the UK.

What I want you to see here is that there are times when
the seasons of preparation are longer than the moments
themselves.

Once I got to Uganda, the sports ministry was set up
very quickly, and the team that helped me set its
foundation truly owned the moment, as they took high
levels of responsibility upon themselves and were very
proactive in the whole process.[16] As the sports ministry

---

[16] Shout out to Acidri Ephraim for playing a big part in this.

started up so efficiently and effectively, I soon realised that there were more leadership opportunities available to me in Uganda than I first thought.

Some of these opportunities came about naturally, such as church leaders inviting me to go and speak at their services. On the other hand, there were opportunities that were never planned and I would never have been able to see them coming. Life is like this. There will always be moments, seasons and events we could never have predicted in a million years.

To be honest, these unpredictable and unforeseeable moments are often moments of chaos, disruption and pain. While in Uganda, this is exactly what happened to me. I remember waking on one particular morning, simply feeling awful. I felt sick, I was freezing cold and my body ached all over. But what really told me that I wasn't well was my lack of appetite; anyone who knows me will know that this is especially unusual for me.

About half an hour after getting up, I was lying on the sofa hugging my knees like a baby, just trying to keep warm, when I started to be sick. Now I will spare you the details, but my vomit indicated to my Ugandan friends that it was likely I had pretty severe malaria. As a result, I had to be taken to hospital.

By the time I got to hospital, my symptoms were getting worse. When I tried to stand up, I could feel the whole world spinning around me and I felt like I was going to pass out. I couldn't even drink, because whenever I did, it made me throw up again.

The severity of how ill I was really hit me when I went through triage in the hospital. As part of this, they measured my bodyweight. Now, I am not the biggest of guys, my build is quite slim and I don't carry a lot of muscle mass. Usually, I weigh about 70kg; however, I was a long way from that on those hospital scales. I weighed in at 62kg. In one morning of sickness, I had lost 8kg. This was not good.

My symptoms continued to get worse. I threw up all over the hospital floor, and standing up and walking had become so challenging that I had to be taken around in a wheelchair. Having been examined by the doctor, I was told I needed to be kept in the hospital.

The staff were very kind and generous to me, as they accommodated me in a side room on one of the wards to allow me some privacy. This hospital in Uganda was very crowded, as families were required to stay with their sick family members in order to feed them. Furthermore, as this was Africa, you could also expect a rogue chicken to come clucking its way through the hospital wards.

As I was a missionary, the hospital knew people would give me lots of attention, so they placed me in a side room to remove me from all of the hustle and bustle. I remember very clearly sitting in my wheelchair, when the doctors, nurses and my local Ugandan friends discussed in Lugbara (the local language) where to put me. Soon after, my friends pushed me in my wheelchair through the corridors of the hospital before turning up the ramp that led to the ward labelled 'Paediatrics'.

On entering the ward and heading to my allocated side room, I was able to look around the ward. I could see all of the sick children and their families. My heart was broken. Heading into my side room, I felt God whisper into my ear, 'Before you leave this hospital, I want you to go and speak to all of these children and their families.'

Over the next few days, those words whispered into my ear by God were what I held on to as I endured my own sickness. Whenever I threw up, shivered with fever, watched drip after drip of medicine being put in my arm, some of which burned like crazy and caused me more pain than I'd ever felt before (and has had lifelong side effects on my skin), all I thought about was those children. I had to endure it, because I had to speak to them. This was God's promise to me.

After three days in hospital, I was at a point where I could be discharged. I was by no means fully healthy and my body was still weak – it turned out I'd had septicaemia. The doctor had come to see me and wanted to take the cannula from my arm so I could leave the hospital. However, I asked him if I could keep the cannula in my arm because I wanted to go and speak to the children on the ward, and I wanted them to see that I understood what they were going through. He agreed.

Going to speak with the children and their families was one of the most emotional and heart-warming moments of my entire life. Along with my friend Joel, who translated for me, I shared the good news of Jesus with every child and family. At the end of our time we had the whole ward singing and dancing in the local language. It was amazing! You wouldn't have thought anyone on the ward was sick, because there was so much joy present in the moment. As the psalmist says: 'Weeping may stay for the night, but rejoicing comes in the morning' (Psalm 30:5).

Even when you feel like a moment is kicking you in the butt, you can still own it! No matter what the situation, you can own the moment in the bad and the good. *Every moment can be owned, if you have the courage to take the lead.*

Owning the moment will require you to step out and give 100 per cent to what you are facing in the present, because without giving the moment the attention it deserves, you may miss the gold in what is in front of you.

I love the story of the creation in Genesis 1, the first book of the Bible. I believe that there are some key fundamentals of owning the moment in what we see God do throughout this story. Here are four points of application demonstrated by God in Genesis 1 that you too can apply to your everyday life in order to truly own the moment.

1. Work like a workhorse

What I love about the creation story most is how God literally left nothing out. For those six days, God worked hard on His creation and used all of His creative imagination as He spoke the earth and life into being. He gave 100 per cent effort in creating the world we now inhabit. Furthermore, as part of creation, He made humans, the most unique invention in history. God worked so hard on creation that He cared about the small details just as much as the big details. He knew that the *small* details are just as important as the *big* ones.

If we are to own the moment in leadership, we too must be prepared to give 100 per cent effort in all the areas in which we are working. Like God, we must care about the *small* details just as much as the *big* ones. *To truly own the moment, you must see every moment as of equal importance and significance.* In doing so, you will create an atmosphere where you can fully invest in every person you meet and every task you do – now, that is owning the moment!

2. Celebrate like a champion

One of the greatest parts in the story is how God daily looks at His new creation and repeatedly sees that it 'was good'.[17] God takes time to celebrate what He has created. There are many leaders I know who never take proper time to celebrate their moments of success. They complete one task or finish a season of life and they are in a rush to move quickly on to what is next.

If you live like this in leadership, you will swiftly start to suck away all of the joy that comes from leading people. Taking moments to celebrate in your leadership, even if the moments appear small, will dramatically add to the joy and gratitude you have. This, in turn, will give you more energy and a stronger desire to keep going for the long haul.

It is too easy to let a moment pass you by and miss the glory found in it. By taking the time to reflect, you create space to celebrate like a champion and give yourself permission to grab all of the gold out of the moment. Don't let a positive moment pass you by without taking time to celebrate it. By taking this time to celebrate, you will find the gold in every moment and every person.

3. Communicate like a counsellor

Also seen in the story of creation is the first-ever conversation. A conversation between Father, Son and Holy Spirit who decide to make human beings in their image (Genesis 1:26-27). To own a moment will require

---

[17] See Genesis 1:4,10,12,18,21,25,31.

clear and strong communication with those around you, especially with those you are leading.

Naturally, there are two sides to communication: listening and speaking. Both will be required to own a moment. *To truly listen means you are able to take in all the information around you.* By taking in this information, you then have the ability to act, based upon what you have heard or seen.

A good counsellor will always listen before they speak. They will listen to every detail in order to formulate the most effective and appropriate response to the person under their care. As leaders who are going to own the moment, we too must be prepared to listen and take in *all* the information around us before we speak or act. Listening well always helps a leader to make better decisions in any moment.

4. Rest like a reservoir

I spoke about prioritising rest earlier, but that does not mean it isn't worth mentioning again. Rest is essential if you are going to own the moment effectively and frequently. Even at the beginning of time, God saw this to be true. Having created the world, God Himself decided to rest and take time away from working.

Now, there are two aspects of rest when it comes to owning the moment. The first is the principle that taking time to rest will refuel your energy and give you greater focus to see the world around you so you can own the moments you are presented with.

The second principle of rest and owning the moment is to see rest itself as a moment you can own. As with giving work 100 per cent, we also need to give rest the same level of investment. That means taking rest seriously. Rest time is time to guard and protect, but also, rest is time to enjoy. So as you plan your time, don't just put in guarded time to rest; also give space for activities you enjoy and find beauty in.

When you look at a reservoir, there is something beautiful and special about the stillness of the water. Similarly, there is beauty for us in our times of rest. The water held in a reservoir is not active and running ferociously all the time, and neither should we. Take time to stop. See rest itself as a time to own and you too will find the beauty in resting like a reservoir.

Summary: *By working hard, celebrating your wins, talking with and listening to others and taking time to rest, you will be able to own every moment in life. If you have the courage, you will be able to step out whenever there is a moment that calls for a leader who is willing to take the lead. So, when the moment arises, own it!*

16
Facing Opposition

Your greatest opportunity could present your
greatest opposition.

As my time in Uganda was coming to a close, I was invited to speak at a large-scale conference a few months later. Consequently, I returned home to the UK and got straight on to preparing a short two-week trip back to Uganda a few months later, to speak at the conference.

The conference took place over four days and saw some of the best and most mature speakers in Uganda and parts of the Democratic Republic of the Congo invited to speak, as well as myself. All of the other speakers were twice my age, highly experienced and far more qualified than me; they also held highly esteemed positions of leadership. I was pinching myself and couldn't help but feel somewhat intimidated by the position I found myself in. I was also extremely excited by the unique opportunity. I couldn't wait to speak!

The conference came around and I did everything I could to take in my surroundings. At the start of every day and at lunchtime, all of the speakers would line up behind a brass band and marching brigade who would play and process to the conference area. As we processed, we would walk through the large crowd of 20,000 people to our seats by the main stage.

The atmosphere was electric. People danced and cheered loudly as the procession walked past them. There was clear anticipation of a life-changing four days ahead for those attending.

For the first two and a half days I watched from my seat by the stage as the atmosphere of the crowd increased session by session, as the highly established Ugandan and Congolese speakers spoke with such eloquence and with vast knowledge on their topics and Bible passages. I marvelled as I watched these men and women do their thing.

Then it was my turn to speak.

I had been given many opportunities to speak in public before this conference, especially during my seven months in Uganda, but having watched all the other speakers do such a great job, I felt intimidated by the task at hand. Thankfully, it was the lunch break before my speaking session, which meant I was able to call my uncle Jeff back in the UK to pray for me before I went to speak. His prayer was a huge help and reassurance.

However, my unease soon returned as the time came for the procession back to the conference. This unease was not caused by having to talk, but rather because something was missing in the procession. Whenever the processions took place, all the speakers would walk together at the back of the procession. On this occasion, I was the only speaker there. None of the other speakers wanted to walk with me.

It seemed the majority of the other speakers were against me speaking. It appeared they did not believe that someone so young should really be able to speak at such an event. I also discovered that the speakers and some of the other organisers of the conference had apparently tried to prevent me from speaking; when I had arrived in Uganda, I actually wasn't on the programme. Sadly, I heard there had been many devaluing and harsh words said about me behind my back.

Once the procession arrived at the conference area, I could see the other speakers already there. As I headed towards my seat, none of them looked at me; instead, they all stared at the ground or straight past me.

I was so alone. Here I was, about to speak in front of 20,000 people and it felt like barely anyone was willing to support me.

Sadly, you will always face opposition in leadership, especially when you are young. People will often look down on you, expect little of you, disrespect you and sometimes speak down to you. In moments like these, your responses are crucial. *How you respond to negativity will showcase the true depth of your character.*

Despite the harsh opposition I faced in Uganda, I knew I had a choice around how I responded. I could have got angry or bitter, I could have started bad-mouthing the other speakers in return. I could have decided not to speak and run away from the uncomfortable and daunting scenario I found myself in.

It is often easier to run away, but – as I have said earlier in this book – just because something is *easier* doesn't mean that it's *better*. Good leaders will do all that they can to choose the better option as opposed to the easier one, even in the face of opposition.

As the air of opposition rose for me in Uganda, I was determined not to give up. I knew God had given me a message to share with all those at the conference. Despite my young age and what everyone was saying, I knew God had called me to own this moment and take the lead.

Here are the steps I took to meet the opposition I was facing. These are general steps, and they are all steps you can take yourself.

1. Embrace grace

Grace, which is modelled to us best by Jesus, is a principle whereby we treat others with love regardless of how they treat us. When people treat us badly, our worldly opinion says that they do not *deserve* for us to treat them well in response. Grace, however, would choose to love someone even if they did not deserve it.

At the conference, although the other speakers did not even want to look at me, I still went up to them, shook their hands, said hello and asked how they were doing – this was the usual protocol in the Ugandan culture.

Although this may seem like a simple thing to do, it is not straightforward. This is not because of the actions taken, but rather owing to the motives at play on the inside. To truly embrace grace and treat those who oppose you with grace, it requires the right heart posture. If I had shaken the hands of the other speakers while I was angry and bitter at their actions towards me, this would not have been grace-full. However, if I shook their hands having forgiven them for their actions and out of a place of love, then that would be.

If you are able to lead while embracing grace, every bit of opposition you face will make you better and not bitter. This will allow you to lead with freedom, taking away any pressure that you could feel as a result of others' resistance. Leading with such freedom will give you the space to embrace other key ingredients you will need to take the lead and deal with any opposition that may come your way.

2. Engage courage

When facing any opposition, it can be a challenge to keep going. Like I said, it would have been easy for me to run away from speaking at the conference. If you are going to move forward, which a good leader will aim to do, it will require courage to do so.

I remember the master of ceremonies calling my name. It was my time to speak. I walked up the mountain of steps on to the stage with my translator, Joel, right behind me. As we got up on the stage, I could see all of the 20,000 people waiting expectantly. Looking round, it took me a moment to take it all in; I mean, 20,000 is a lot of people!

I took a deep breath, said a prayer and began to speak.

What I noticed here, as I have noticed in other courageous moments, is that the hardest step is the first one. Once you take the first step and the process gets going, your confidence begins to grow, as does the amount of courage.

As I got deeper into my talk, I had a crazy idea. I decided to speak one of the lines in my talk in the local

Lugbara language. Incredibly, the cheers when I did it were the biggest of the conference! But the important point here is that confidence and courage grow, once you take the first step – a step you may need to take a few times as you face different situations.

3. Embody humility

Once you overcome opposition, the feeling of relief is huge. I was overwhelmingly at peace once I sat back in my seat after giving my talk. However, I did not expect what happened next.

The final speaker of the day stepped onto the stage. As he began, he referred back to my talk, with high praise. I was quite blown away by the kindness and magnitude of his comments.

While it is of course very affirming to receive such praise, there is also a need to be humble in receiving it. Similar to being grace-full, humility requires the right heart posture to be done well.

Having faced opposition, receiving high praise could leave us wanting to rub the other person's face in our success. This is not leadership. The example of a good leader would be to receive this praise with gratitude and humility. What this means is that we will allow the praise to give us confidence, but we will not allow it to increase our ego, or cause us to fall into cockiness.

The best way to do this is to thank someone for their praise and leave it at that. That is how a leader embodies humility.

Summary: Opposition is inevitable, especially in leadership and in those big moments when you are taking the lead. However, how you respond to the opposition is completely up to you. The best leaders will respond with grace, courage and humility. Taking these steps will ultimately allow you to complete the task that God has for you to fulfil.

17
Communication Skills

Your level of influence will be determined by your
ability to communicate.

Following my time in Uganda, I returned home to the UK
and started working as a physiotherapist. The company I
worked for was run by a friend of mine, Dan, whom I had
previously worked with during my days in football. Dan
was a great guy to work for. He was generous,
accommodating and he had a big vision for the growth of
the business. Having an extra member of staff enabled him
to work towards this.

I really enjoyed the job. Although there were some very
long days in a small treatment room, the patients were
generally easy-going and a joy to work with. Naturally,
though, some patients were not as straightforward. This
could have been because of the nature of the condition
they needed treatment for, or as a result of emotional
difficulties they were facing at the time. And on some
occasions, patients simply did not like the treatment they
were being given; it's like the restaurant equivalent of
having food sent back.

Moments like these call for inner strength in order to take the lead effectively.

No matter what role you are in, you will always have to work with people. Sadly, this is not always straightforward. However, working as a physiotherapist taught me the fundamental skills of communication. When dealing with someone's emotions or their complaints, how you communicate in return is very important and will show what kind of a leader you are.

Here are some key fundamentals of strong communication, which will help you take the lead.

1. Authenticity in listening

As a physiotherapist, or any other medical professional, before you can treat a patient you are required to ask some questions to get an idea of what the problem may be. The answers to the questions will lead the medical professional to particular physical assessments before finally providing the appropriate treatment.

Through the whole assessment process, the greatest skill a medical professional must have is the ability to listen. Don't get me wrong, they must also know their anatomy and have a good understanding of medical conditions, of course, but *without being able to listen effectively, it is difficult to achieve the best results and reach the correct conclusions.*

I will never forget one patient I had as a physiotherapist. This person had come to see me with back pain. They had a long medical history, with a variety of ongoing medical conditions. In hearing their medical history, it was very clear to me that they had felt very disappointed by medical professionals in the past and carried the emotional pain of feeling like no one was prepared to listen to them.

Now, in normal circumstances, when someone comes to see a physiotherapist, they are assessed, treated and usually provided with some exercises to do at home. However, I realised that this conventional route needed some modifying for this particular patient.

So, instead of giving them lots of exercises and doing lots of hands-on treatment, I decided that the best thing to do was to sit and listen to them. For all of their treatment sessions, the patient came in, and we chatted. They told me all about their life. I would listen, and at the end of each session, I would encourage the patient to go for a walk every day of the next week.

Despite me doing very little 'physiotherapy', this patient's back pain went away by the end of their allocated sessions. Really, what this person needed most wasn't physiotherapy, but someone to listen. It was only through listening to their story that I could see what this person really needed.

If you want to make the best leadership decisions, you first need to listen to people. Sometimes, *taking* the lead looks like *giving* the lead. You need to give others the space to be heard. Listening gives this space. It allows people to feel valued, important and wanted, especially in a team. But what this story has also shown is that good listening has the capability to facilitate inner healing.

2. Sensitivity in speaking

I'm sure that when most of you saw the title of this chapter the first thought that popped into your mind was about speaking. Speaking is a crucial communicative skill in leadership. However, it is vital to understand that *the best speakers are the best listeners.* You can't speak with sensitivity without listening.

Communication is two-way. There is listening and there is speaking – although, in my mind, the best speaking occurs when listening is also present. Let me explain what I mean. If someone who did lots of public speaking came to a youth event and started speaking about 'How God can use you in your retirement', I am not sure the message would be well received. The person speaking may be incredibly gifted at communicating, but I would say that this person is a good *presenter*, not a good *speaker*, because the best speakers are the best listeners. For someone to be a good speaker, they must listen to what is around them, as listening gives them knowledge of what they need to speak into.

If our speaker came to the youth event and spoke on the subject of 'How God can use young people in their schools', this would show that they were a good listener. It would show they had listened to what the event was all about and it would give an indication that they had listened to young people by talking about a subject they are interested in.

This is the difference between gifted *presenters* and gifted *speakers* – speakers take time to listen before they speak.

Whenever you find yourself taking the lead, I encourage you to listen before you speak. I recently read a story about a business leader who, during team meetings, would let everyone else in the team speak before they would.[18] Their listening determined what they said in response. It meant their response was in line with what the team were saying, meaning the team understood the leader's language.

I believe everyone has the ability to speak, but it is great listeners who make the greatest speakers. As you take the lead, make sure you take time to listen, and then your words will be filled with power and authority, no matter how many people you are speaking in front of.

3. Clarity in decision-making

Listening and speaking work in partnership when it comes to bringing clarity in making decisions. You can't have one without the other, otherwise clarity will be lost. Listening allows you to take in and make sense of the information and the thoughts of others around you. Speaking allows you to showcase that you have listened and gives volume to your decisions when taking the lead.

Anyone listening to a leader desires clarity. Therefore, make your responses, instructions and desires simple. Provide information that people will understand. If your decisions are showcased with clarity, it will empower others to do what they need to do with the bigger picture in mind and with a confidence that what they are doing is right and valued by the leader.

---

[18] See Simon Sinek, *Leaders Eat Last* (New York: Penguin, 2017), p 219.

4. Creativity in everything

Finally, with every aspect of communication, it is important to note that every person is different. While the three points above are generally the same for everyone, the specificity of them all may differ for each person. For example, some people may like to listen, whereas others may best receive information through the written word. This is a simple example, but the point is that people are different.

As a result, you will need to get creative in your communication. This may be through using pictures, films or practical illustrations. Whatever it is, it is only effective if the other person gets your message. Be willing to try out any means of communication possible. There is no limit on creativity so try as much as you can and you'll find out what works for those in your sphere of influence.

Summary: *Your level of influence will be determined by your ability to communicate. To maximise influence, all areas of communication must be adhered to, as all link together. Listening helps take in the world around you, to enable you to produce the best spoken response and communicate your decisions with clarity. But don't forget that everyone is different and will have varying communication preferences. Therefore, make sure you are willing to get creative in your communication.*

Part summary

It takes courage to take the lead, but every moment calls for someone who is willing to put themselves out there and own the moment. No matter your age or experience, that courage is inside you. You can take the lead. Admittedly, taking the lead is not always easy. There will be opposition and challenges that come your way, but that's exactly why it takes courage – if it was easy, you wouldn't need courage. So take courage and take the lead; this moment needs you!

Part Four
Helping Others to Lead

A good leader doesn't aim to make more followers; a good leader helps to make more leaders. This final section of the book will help you see how you can use influence and leadership positions to create new leaders and develop existing ones. If we are really serious about wanting to be the kind of leader who will change the world, it is only through equipping others to lead that it will be possible, because the more effective leaders there are in the world, the more positive influence there will be as a result.

18
Taking Others on the Journey

Let others in on what you've got.

My university lecturer Chris Duffett often says that 'we need to let others in on what we've got'. In saying this, Chris is referring to sharing the faith and relationship that we have in and with Jesus. Chris is coming from a belief that having a relationship with Jesus is the best news ever, and therefore we should want to share this with whoever we can, because it is that good!

Similarly, as leaders we should look to let others in on the influence we've got. Now, what is important here is to understand that we are not trying to get people to have influence in the same *area* as us, but at the same *level* as us. Like we have shown many times in this book, people are all different, so therefore their potential sphere of influence will be different. When we are trying to help and build up new, influential leaders, we have to enable them to have influence in whatever spheres they are in.

This is what I tried to do with my brother Matty, when we went on a short overseas mission trip to Kenya.

Following my trip to Uganda, word had somehow reached Kenya about the work I had been doing. As a result, I received a message from a man called Wachira about heading to a place called Kibera. Kibera is positioned on the outskirts of Nairobi and is statistically the largest slum area in all of Africa, with a population of 700,000 people.[19] After many discussions with Wachira and lots of prayer, it was clear that God was calling me to head out to Kenya for a short period of time.

Although I had been invited by Wachira and his team, I was determined not to go alone. I wanted someone else to have an opportunity to learn from the experience as well as myself. It just so happened that the trip fitted in with my brother Matty's diary. Matty was doing his GCSEs that year, which meant he finished school earlier than everyone else and therefore had time available.

When asked if he wanted to join me in Kenya, Matty said 'Yes' straight away, despite being warned of the difficulties he would face working in a slum environment – I have always been inspired by his courage and desire to help others, even as a young person.

However, knowing Matty was coming with me did mean I had to make sure certain things were in place. I wanted him to have the best possible experience to help him grow, but I also wanted him to enjoy it. And because he is my brother, I wanted to ensure he was going to be as safe as possible.

Whenever you invite anyone to come with you on the leadership journey, whether that takes you away from

[19] www.weforum.org/agenda/2016/10/these-are-the-worlds-five-biggest-slums (accessed 6th August 2022).

home or not, the spaces you create for growth, joy and safety are vitally important. Here is how you can do this, along with how these played out with Matty in Kenya.

1. Create space for their gifting

You can't help someone understand influence without giving them space to use their gifting. Naturally, the place where people will have most influence is within the realms of their own abilities. Therefore, when helping others to lead, it is vital that you create space for them to use their own gifting.

Matty has many gifts, but one of the unique giftings he had coming into our trip to Kenya was the ability to lead marching drills. Matty had been a member of the Air Cadets all through his early teenage years and had a few years' experience of marching drills. He was clearly gifted in this area, because he kept getting promoted to different ranks within the Cadets.

As this was one of his gifts, I sought out ways he might be able to use this in Kenya. In discussion with Wachira, it turned out that one of the local churches in Kibera had a Boys' and Girls' Brigade that often performed marching activities at church services and other events. Being able to march is a key skill that any Brigade member will continually work on. So this opened a door and provided a space in our schedule in Kibera for Matty to go through some marching drills and games with the boys and girls in one of the Brigades in Kibera.

Matty really excelled in leading the session. I simply watched and took pictures as he led them through various drills and games. The boys and girls laughed and were clearly filled with joy throughout, and they were all desperate for a photograph to be taken with Matty. Clearly, they responded well to his leadership, and positive influence was achieved.

Had the schedule just been filled with things to fit in with my gifting, we would never have visited the Brigade. This again helps to show that if you can create space for others to use their gifting, you can grow a new leader and increase the positive influence around the world in ways that you couldn't do just by yourself.

2. Create space for reflection

Matty really flourished during our time in Kibera. In every activity where he was leading, whether that be the Brigade or helping me with sports for the children, he excelled. However, despite flourishing, Kibera was a tough place to visit, especially for someone who had never been to Africa before. The sights Matty was exposed to were sights he'd never seen in his lifetime. It was a different world from what he was used to.

I knew this would be the case before the trip and I wanted to be prepared for the possible mental challenges Matty could face. Like I said, I wanted him to be safe, and that was not just physically, but mentally and emotionally as well.

When planning the schedule with Wachira before we went to Kibera, I made sure that it had lots of space where no activities were planned, particularly in the evenings. I wanted this space because I wanted to give Matty time for reflection and conversation. If there was anything he had seen that had touched a nerve or something culturally that put his mind in a spin, I wanted him to have a safe space, away from anyone else, where he could talk about it.

So while we were having our evenings in the hotel, eating our meal or just chilling in our room, we would talk about everything we had been exposed to in the day, whether that be through the activities we had put on, the homes we had visited, the sights we had seen just walking around or the conversations we had had with people. We spoke about it all in a very open and honest way.

Every leader needs to reflect, no matter how long they have been in leadership and regardless of how big their influence is. Giving Matty this space to reflect allowed him to grow in confidence in his leadership and created a greater sense of comfort in his unfamiliar surroundings. As the two weeks in Kibera went by, I saw Matty change day by day. He was growing with every bit of exposure he had. But I could only see that because there was space to reflect. Those daily conversations showed me Matty's new levels of confidence and leadership understanding.

If you are going to help others to lead, you need to give them space to reflect. This helps them to get rid of any baggage they may pick up along the way, but it will also help you to monitor their progress and see first-hand how they are growing.

3. Create space for fun

One of the traps that many people fall into in leadership is working too hard for too long. As we saw earlier, rest is really important for leaders. What is also important, amid these times of rest, is time for fun. *Leadership can be a very tiring process if fun is taken out of the equation.*

When you are helping others to lead, I believe it is important that you teach this very early on. I have seen far too many leaders get to a point of no return, where they have been sucked in by leadership to the degree where there is no longer time or space for fun or joy in life. If you are young in your leadership, please create space for fun now, before it's too late.

For me, influence and fun should go together. In fact, if you look at the word influence, you can see that fun and influence actually intertwine:

in F l U e N c e

Having positive influence is amazing, but it does take vast amounts of energy, whereas simply having fun breathes life and energy back into you, which benefits your influence in the long run.

In Kibera, I made sure that Matty and I had a day off from all of our activities, simply so that we could have fun for a day. When I say fun, I basically mean giving ourselves the licence to be typical tourists. We roamed the markets, bought ourselves a Kenyan national football shirt and a cap made of colourful African material each, and went to the supermarket and filled our basket with juice and sweets.

The sweets were incredible! They were yoghurt-based, with a wide variety of flavours, all of which we instantly loved – to be honest, we demolished the whole bag in an afternoon, they were so good! We laughed for hours on that day off and took some of the best selfies. It rejuvenated us and refilled us with joy for our final few days of activities in Kibera.

You will *help others lead by helping them have fun.* After all, no one is going to want to come on a journey with a leader who is too intense and can't have a laugh. Create space for fun. It will aid your influence, but it will also grow the relationship you have with those you are trying to enable to lead.

Matty and I have always been close, but that trip to Kibera took our relationship to a whole new level. Leading together, having space for reflective conversations and having lots of fun gave us brotherly memories for a lifetime. But more importantly, it was life-changing for Matty.

He became more confident. He threw himself into new opportunities with open arms. He even gave a forty-five-minute presentation at Air Cadets all about the trip to Kibera. This is what happens when you help others to lead: they learn how to have influence and become greater influencers themselves. Influence isn't something you do, it's something you carry with you.

So, please, create space to *let others in on what you've got* and help them carry influence themselves.

Summary: *If you are going to take others on the journey towards a life of leadership and influence, you need to give them space. Space to use the gifts that they have, because part of their influence will always be connected to their gifting. Space to reflect, because reflection helps alleviate baggage and helps you to get a first-hand view of their growth. And space for fun, because anyone who is going to have influence must remember that fun and influence are intertwined.*

19
Know Your People

You can't help people lead until you fully know them.

A few months after the short trip to Kenya, I was still working as a physiotherapist, when I was offered a new job. The job involved leading the children's, youth and community outreach work within my church. I had grown up in the church as a teenager and still had some investment from afar into the youth there when I was away at university. As a result, I was excited by the prospect of the role and the further opportunities to invest in all the young people.

One of the main aims of the role was to see the youth take steps into leadership. This particularly excited me, as I am driven by the vision of seeing others reach their full God-given potential and living out the 'greater things' (see John 14:12) God has in store for them.

Through the different leadership positions and spheres of influence I have had, it has always been clear that there is a direct correlation between how well you know people and their growth.

You can't help people lead until you fully know them. When I worked in football, every team manager always said the same thing to me whenever I started: 'Get to know the players.' These managers understood that if I was going to help these players reach their maximal performance and potential, I was going to have to know what made each of them tick.

As I entered into the new job at the church, I knew my first step in helping the young people move into and grow in leadership was to develop a strong relationship with each of them.

Jesus' parable of the wise and foolish builders in the Bible teaches us the importance of laying down strong foundations. In this story (see Matthew 7:24-27), there are two men who each build a house. One builds his house on the sand and the other builds his house on the rock. Later, when a storm comes, the man who built his house on the sand sees his home crumble, whereas the man who built his house on the rock sees his home stand firm despite the force of the storm.

Similarly, when we get to know people, it establishes strong foundations through relationship with them, which creates a platform by which they can step into leadership and be sustained for the long haul.

Getting to know your people comes by using your senses. You have to take in all that is going on around you and be extremely observant, all the way from first starting to get to know someone to helping them step into leadership. Getting to know someone never stops, because people are always changing and developing. Therefore, utilising your senses, as illustrated below, should not be a one-time event, but a continuous point of application within your leadership as you teach others to lead.

1. Ears: what can you hear?

Listen to what people are saying, when they are talking among their peers or with the group and in what they say to you. One of the things I have often tried to do to build relationships with the young people in the church youth group is to watch what they are watching. This does two things: first, it helps me understand the world they are part of, as people will naturally try to blend into the culture around them. Second, it provides me with opportunities to talk about something they are interested in.

I quickly learned that a good number of our church youth group are big fans of the *Marvel* films. As a result, I set out to watch all the films and series that were released on Disney+ to create a foundation for myself to further develop my relationship with them. The more you have to talk about with people, the more you get to know them and what makes them tick.

Additionally, listening helps you pick up clues which you can use to detect what steps may be appropriate for this individual or group to move into leadership. During the COVID-19 pandemic lockdown, like many other churches, our church was doing services on Zoom. As part of these services, we decided to do a youth takeover Sunday, where the youth would lead every part of the meeting.

Doing things on Zoom provided two options for the youth leading the service: they could either do the service live and in the moment, or they could pre-record each component and simply play the service as a video. The youth told me that they wanted to pre-record each part, as they felt there would be less pressure than having to do it live on an online platform.

Our leadership team listened to their preference and all the youth who participated did a wonderful job. Had we not listened to the youth, we may have put too much pressure on them, which may have caused them to be over-anxious and not lead as well as they did. Make sure you listen to the feelings of others, because no matter how well you think you know them, people will always know themselves better than you do.

2. Eyes: what can you see?

If you have ever been part of a group or team for any length of time, you will have seen how people naturally form sub-groups within larger groups. These smaller groups are often called cliques. The word 'cliques' may make you think of dining hall scenes in films or TV shows, with all the different groups of people sat in different places from one another.

While we don't want to see cliques in the groups we lead, as we want to see unity, seeing the cliques or friendships within the larger group can be useful in helping others to lead. This is because two friends taking steps to lead together is more likely to happen than one person on their own.

For another church service on Zoom, I asked two young people to give a short talk. It was the first time either of them had done anything like this. However, these two people were from the same friendship group. As a result, they worked together on the talk by sharing ideas and encouraging one another. When they came to do the talk, both had some nerves, but they championed one another like true friends do and spoke incredibly well. I was glad I had seen their close friendship, as it proved to help their step into leadership.

There will of course, be many other things that you can see with your eyes. One thing that cliques make very obvious is the people who are always left out. These people need your attention. So take note of what you see and it will inform your decision-making as a leader and when helping others to lead.

3. Touch: do they need affirmation?

Using touch when you are in a position of leadership can have very positive effects – as long as it is done within appropriate parameters. Sadly, there have been far too many leaders who have been abusive with the sense of touch and damaged those they should have been caring for.

However, I can't endorse a fist bump enough – especially if you want to look like you've got some street cred. But also, a fist bump does a great job in affirming to someone that they have done something well and that you are proud of them. I have found a simple fist bump has been effective in building relationships with young people in church and other areas of society, especially during team-based activities.

Everyone needs to know that someone is on their side. Some people will not take the first steps into leadership alone – they need someone alongside them, some affirmation. A casual fist bump could help them to see that you are this person.

4. Voice: what response do you get?

Like with touch, using your voice should be appropriate, as the tongue can build up and destroy; it can be a source for good or evil (James 3:10). Good leaders will use their words to encourage and build people up and act as a source of support. They will also ask good questions during a discussion.

Observing how people respond to your voice will give you a good sense of how they perceive their relationship with you and if they have understood what you have said.

I regularly tell the young people in our youth group that they have value, but it was only recently I knew that they had taken in this truth. One of the girls in the group wrote me a card, which simply said, 'Thank you for valuing us.' It was a precious moment, as it highlighted that she was truly hearing and understanding what I was saying to the whole group.

Helping others to lead will require the same process. There will be times when you speak life into people, but they won't get it. Keep going, though, because there will be a time when they do get it, like the girl who gave me the card. Once they do understand what you are saying about them, that is the moment when you know they trust you. And once they trust you, then you can more easily take someone on the journey to stepping into and growing in leadership and influence.

Use your voice, watch the response and let it show you what your group know and what they don't know. Either way, you have a foundation to build on.

Summary: *To get to know people, you need to use your senses and adequately take in what is going on around you. By doing so, you will be able to fully get to know those you are leading and be best educated to help them step into and advance their leadership.*

20
Baggage vs Luggage

*You can't choose your scars, but you can choose
how you carry them.*

About nine months into my job leading the youth at the
church, life took a number of unexpected turns as a result
of the coronavirus lockdowns. One consequence was the
cancellation of all school and college exams. Working with
young people, I saw first-hand how mentally challenging
this was for them to deal with. After all, many of them had
worked so hard to prepare. Having them taken away in a
quick-fire, two-minute government announcement on the
television was a heart-breaking moment for many young
people, which was then followed by a difficult time in
lockdown, having to deal with the pain and grief of feeling
like all their hard work was for nothing. Let alone the
isolation.

In crisis moments like these, people look to leaders for
stability, direction, comfort and inspiration, which makes
these moments key when teaching others how to lead,
because people are watching you. They are seeing how
you may be able to journey with them through the storm

and, ultimately, they will learn a lot from you about leadership through this season of pain.

There are many skills we spoke about in the 'Communication Skills' chapter, such as listening authentically and speaking with sensitivity, which will be helpful here. But, essentially, what people are really wanting from a leader is to know that everything is going to be OK. They want to know that there will be a way through and out of the pain.

While you can say and do all the right things here – you can give great words of wisdom and sound advice, you can make people laugh and feel good for a moment, you can listen with every ounce of attentive energy you've got – none of this will quite be enough for what those you are leading desire from you.

This is where there is power in your story and the scars you have collected from personal experiences of pain, disappointment and heartbreak. *Your story has the potential to connect with people in the midst of their pain.* However, how comfortable you feel about sharing the scars from your seasons of pain will depend on one key question: do you see them as baggage or luggage?

When getting ready to fly on holiday, I enjoy getting everything I need into my suitcase – and once my mum has checked I haven't forgotten anything, I'm good to go. I know some people don't like packing, but for me, I get excited thinking about what I'm going to pack, because I can't help but let my mind wonder about all the holiday fun I'm going to have with those items. In a nutshell, luggage is exciting and useful – everywhere you take it!

Baggage, on the other hand, doesn't sound so much fun. It sounds heavy, and straight away infers that there is something weighing us down. Many people view their painful or shameful past as baggage. They see their past hurts and disappointments as a brick wall that is impossible to get over, under, or even around. Essentially, however you view baggage, it is almost always associated with an inability to shake off the past and move forward into the future.

A question you may ask here, is: how can you determine whether your painful experiences are baggage or luggage? Simply, painful seasons can be identified as *luggage* when they no longer have a negative impact on you – you may even feel gratitude and joy as you look back at the situation. You will find yourself in a mindset where you feel comfortable to reveal, discuss and use those areas of pain.

Alternatively, if something is an item of *baggage*, you would feel apprehensive and uncomfortable at the idea of passing it through the baggage scanner of life, where it could be exposed to the eyes of the world. There will be a sense of holding back and not exposing the areas of pain associated with baggage, whereas with luggage there will be no holding back, as you see your scars as useful, particularly for those you are leading and helping to lead.

If someone does share their pain while it is still baggage, it will come from a place of insecurity and be portrayed in a negative way. When the pain is luggage, it is shared from a place of security.

It's OK if you feel aspects of pain and want to hold back some areas, because it shows there is still a need for some inner healing. *Going through the healing process is what allows baggage to turn into luggage.* This can take time, but getting to a point where you feel comfortable with sharing your areas of pain is one of the greatest aspects of freedom you will ever feel – even if it takes some boldness to get the words out.

We all have scars – no one is immune to them – but the beauty of a scar is that *scars show when a healing process is complete.* They show when a wound has fully healed. They indicate when pain is no longer baggage but luggage. It's here that we find true freedom as we vulnerably share our seasons of pain with others as a means to connect with them and be an example in leadership.

So, once something is luggage, you become comfortable to reveal, discuss and use what you have been through. Here is how that can look, along with how it played out for me while leading the young people through their pain and grief of no exams during lockdown.

1. Comfortable to reveal

Something amazing happens when you are brave enough to reveal past areas of pain to others: it proves that you are a miracle. As soon as you reveal what you have been through, it automatically makes people think about you a little differently. There is an inner response of new-found respect which they now have for you, along with validation to any words of comfort that you may share.

I love being able to share past experiences with the young people I am privileged to lead, not least because of the perplexed look on their faces when I tell them what I have been through. It is as if they see the past version of me and then the current version of me sat beside them, and it causes some confusion. They see the two versions of me as two completely different people. This is why I love revealing past pain and mistakes – it clearly demonstrates change and growth.

Too often, leaders will shy away from sharing their own past hurts or mistakes. But what I have learned is that as soon as you get comfortable revealing what you have been through, you prove that growth is possible to those you are leading. After all, if people are following you, it is because they want to grow. So let your baggage become luggage and get comfortable revealing what you have been through, because those you are leading need to see that growth is possible.

As the young people experienced their exam heartbreak, I did an exercise with them where they wrote down all the painful experiences they themselves had been through, having first revealed all of mine to them. Then, on the back of the piece of paper, I got them to write down how they felt they had grown through all these situations, again having first demonstrated this in areas of my own life.

By sharing my experiences with the young people and through doing the exercise, there was a clear release of hope that spread throughout the group. One of the boys even sent me a message to tell me how helpful the session was and how hope-filled he was, coming out of it. Most significantly, though, he told me how he was able to go through what we had done with his friends. He was influenced and then became the influencer.

2. Comfortable to discuss

It is one thing to simply reveal what you have been through; it is another thing entirely to get comfortable with discussing it. Any discussion involves questions, meaning that in the atmosphere of a conversation, anyone could ask you anything about what you have revealed. As a result, the intricate and deep details of your story could be exposed.

I would advise you to keep discussions about certain things to a one-on-one mentoring setting, mainly because I believe that deeper topics are most effectively spoken through one to one. Discussion can bring about connection and build relationship in a very unique way. Discussing things with someone individually, allowing them to ask questions, will bring about greater depth in sharing; elements of their current pain will connect to your story. This is likely to be very different from what you might share in a larger group setting.

The idea of letting someone ask you questions about your painful moments may seem a bit overwhelming, but it is a very good indicator for you on a personal level to discern what parts of your story are luggage and what may still be baggage. However, nothing will ever grow your relationship with those you are leading faster than a deep and vulnerable conversation. What is more, *vulnerability often produces vulnerability*. This means that those you are talking with are more likely to share the deep parts of their current pain, which will be of great benefit to them.

3. Comfortable to use

Jesus showed what it looks like to be comfortable to use your scars, after He resurrected from the dead. When the disciples were locked in a room together, Jesus appeared to them. However, at this initial appearing, Thomas was not with the other disciples. On hearing what had happened from the other disciples, Thomas doubted – clearly he had some trust issues with the rest of the group. In fact, Thomas said that he would only believe that Jesus had risen if he was able to touch the scars from the nails that had held Jesus' body on the cross (see John 20:25).

One day, while all the disciples were together, including Thomas, Jesus again appeared to them. In this famous scene, Jesus showed Thomas His scars and even allowed him to touch them. This was exactly what Thomas needed to turn his doubt to belief (see John 20:26-29).

When you use your scars to help others, the same exchange takes place. The doubts people have of a better tomorrow can be taken away and replaced with a hope for the future. That is the beauty that comes when you carry your scars as luggage – you can use them to stir up hope in those you are leading.

Sometimes, *teaching others to lead is simply about being a model through your own pain and suffering*, because the reactions, responses and grace you show in those moments teach more about leadership than any textbook ever could. One of the greatest lessons you can model to someone is how to carry the scars of life and turn baggage into luggage.

A final thought on baggage and luggage. When your baggage has turned to luggage you have two *free* hands to help others with their baggage. In turn, when you help someone carry their baggage, it gives them a spare hand to help someone else with their baggage too. In other words, they still have one hand on influence and helping others. Now, that is the kind of domino effect we should want to see when we are helping others to lead.

So if you see someone with some baggage, why not say to them, 'Let me help you with that...'

Summary: *Everyone has experienced pain in their lives. How you carry the scars from that pain, though, is up to you. You can either see it as baggage, which will hold you back, or you can see it as luggage, whereby you see all experiences, including the painful ones, as something that can be used in your life and leadership. By modelling this to those you lead, you are modelling to them the power of vulnerability. So see everything as luggage and use your story, because it has power.*

21
Practical Beats Theory

The best way to learn it is to live it.

As coronavirus continued to bring about a long period in lockdown during 2020 and 2021, I found there was much to learn about leadership. It has always struck me how churches particularly love to plan their small group-based teaching around discussion. Creating space for discussion is excellent, as it provides an avenue for questions to be asked and perspectives from a variety of people to be heard.

However, as youth groups went online, via platforms such as Zoom, it quickly became clear that this was not a medium young people liked. Zoom seemed to stir up a multitude of insecurities, including for those in our church youth group. This meant that young people felt uncomfortable about unmuting their microphones for discussion. As a result, how teaching was done needed to be changed. And as it so happened, this was a game-changer.

Through some trial and error, our leadership team soon realised that the young people reacted well to practical activities, which gave them space to think about the topics we were teaching each week. All of the activities had a creative element to them, which played to the strengths of the youth. These activities also helped them to grow in their faith, as it gave them tools to apply their faith in their lives every day – which you don't get when your teaching is solely based around theory.

Seeing the growth in the young people through this time, I truly realised that practical beats theory. While theory has its place in learning, it will never equip someone in the same way as practically living out what they are learning, especially when it comes to faith and when what you are learning about could be used for influence.

To help you see how this happened within our youth group, here are three examples we used to be practical in our teaching and leadership development, based upon some well-known sayings from some of the world's most known brands.

1. *Nike:* **Just Do It**

One of the topics we studied in our youth group, while on Zoom, was generosity. A topic like generosity is particularly limited if you are only going to learn about it theoretically. If you truly want to learn how to be generous, you can't just hear about it, you have to actually do it. That's the only way you will truly learn! In fact, the best way to learn it is to live it.

Seeing this, once lockdown in England ended and restrictions changed, our team planned a summer youth gathering, where the young people could practically learn what it was like to be generous. As a result, we asked all of the young people to design a postcard with a positive message on it. Once they had designed many cards, we posted all the cards in random houses along the road. The young people loved it and were even disappointed when all of the cards had run out.

There is a buzz that comes with influence; our young people had deeply caught that buzz in being generous that day. What's more, the young people asked me weeks later if they could do the activity again in a different road.

If you allow people to practically experience what it is like to lead and be an influence, it is more likely they will catch the buzz that comes with influence and long to do it more. As you help others to lead, don't get too stuck in the theory; allow people to practically *just do it*.

2. *Tesco:* Every Little Helps

Every bit of practical experience is helpful. Therefore, it is important to give people as many opportunities to lead as possible, including different methods, settings and places, as *variety helps people to grow.*

As the UK went into a second coronavirus lockdown, I saw a new opportunity to develop the leadership and influence of the young people in our group. We decided to run a series on social media content called 'Minute Motivations'. 'Minute Motivations' were exactly that: motivating messages that lasted for a minute. A number of the young people recorded themselves sharing a message of motivation, which was then uploaded to the church's social media platforms.

Of course, being an influencer in this way was very different from posting cards. It used other skillsets and conveyed a message using other means of communication and creativity. Some of the ideas the young people came up with were incredible!

The 'Minute Motivations' was a great success, and it even reached other parts of the globe through the powers of social media. However, what was more significant is that it taught the young people that they can be an influence in a variety of ways. Even if it only takes a minute, *every little helps*.

3. *Adidas:* Impossible is Nothing

One of the most limiting factors of trying to teach leadership and influence through theory is that it fails to stir up a belief in people that great things can happen through them. Only through seeing things happen through them can people truly believe that they can be an influencer. It's a bit like science: you can't prove a hypothesis without *doing* the experiment.

This was exactly the case in our youth group; people did not fully think it was possible for great things to happen through them. As a result, we started to lead them through 'faith-building exercises'. These exercises were designed to help the young people to use their imagination in order to encourage someone else in the group. For example, we would get the young people to pray and ask God, 'If the other person was a colour, what colour would best describe them and why?'

At first, the young people did not expect to come up with anything to share with their exercise partner.

However, that was not how it turned out. Each young person delved deeply into their imagination and shared something that was a great blessing and source of encouragement to their partner. As the weeks went by, the efficiency and creative imagination used by the young people in these exercises grew and grew.

What started out as an uncomfortable activity became natural to everyone in the group. A lesson here: *the more you step out of your comfort zone, the bigger your comfort zone will get*.[20] In response to the growth of their comfort zones, it was clear to me that the young people started to see that *impossible is nothing.*

Summary: *If you want to help people to believe that they can be a leader and have influence, you have to show them this through practical exposure. It is only through seeing it for themselves that people will understand their value and influence. Through helping others to see what they can do, you will show them that nothing is impossible!*

---

[20] Shout out to my friend Jess Harrison for helping me with this line.

22

The Value of Mentoring

*We should be mentored ourselves, and we should
also mentor others.*

In Chapter 10, 'Listen to the Right Voices', we considered
some key voices that we all need to listen to. However, one
of the voices we did not mention is the voice of mentors.
Mentors can play a hugely significant role when it comes
to leadership development – both for you personally and
those you are investing into. Like we saw in Chapter 20,
there is something very special about one-on-one
relationships, as they create a depth that you don't get in
a group setting. This helps massively with leadership
development, as a strong relationship is a great
springboard in any mentoring scenario.

As I write this, I have three key people who mentor me
in different ways. I have Jaime, who is a dear friend to me
and supports me through every area of my life and brings
great clarity to my decisions through his deep wisdom.
My friend Greg particularly mentors me in the areas of
evangelism and leadership, by inspiring me through his
own life and asking me the questions that most people

would be scared to ask – we all need a mentor who is prepared to ask these questions. And finally, I have Sarah, who is currently my boss and mentors me through the everyday of working in a church and provides a sharpening effect on all my ideas.

All of my mentors are further on in life and their leadership journey than I am, and they all help me to grow as a disciple of Jesus and make me a better leader through their different perspectives and areas of specialty. Being mentored by these people has been a life-changing experience for me.

However, if we are going to be effective leaders, mentoring should not stop with us. *There should be a flow to mentoring. We should be mentored ourselves, and we should also mentor others.* When there is a flow to mentoring like this, it creates the best possible cycle of leadership development and growth.

So while I am mentored in my own leadership, I also mentor five young people in my church youth group to build them up in their faith and grow them in areas of leadership and influence. Of everything I have ever done in leadership, mentoring is by far the greatest experience and privilege I have had. *I believe there is no greater privilege in leadership than getting a front row seat when watching people grow* – hopefully those who mentor me would say the same. It is mentoring that gives a leader this front row seat opportunity better than anything else.

Hopefully you can see that mentoring is valuable for everyone in leadership, especially when it comes to helping others to grow as leaders. Mentoring has the capacity to add value to people's leadership through many different means. Below are a few characteristics where mentoring really comes into its own.

1. *Training and equipping*

Training and equipping are essential characteristics of mentoring because of their impact on growth. As a leader you will have a toolkit of skills and experiences. These can easily be put to use for the benefit of others, if you make the decision to mentor someone.

The mentoring environment brings forth an opportunity for you to pass on your skills and give advice from your experiences to others. Personally, I love speaking on stages. There is something about planning and putting a talk together that really excites me. However, what I love more is spending time with young people, teaching them the skills of how to prepare a talk and then watching them deliver the talk themselves.

What particularly interests me in the teaching process is seeing how you have to teach people differently. No two people are the same, meaning no two people react in the same way to training, even when it is delivered to them both in the same way. As a mentor, you have to be reactive to those you are leading/mentoring, as this will help you best journey with them as individuals and give you a wider vision of how each of them can be best equipped for influence.

Everyone is gifted and skilled in different ways. Whatever the gifts God has given you, you can be influential in equipping others in those skills and helping them become more mature in their life, leadership and influence.

2. Feedback and reflection

Too often, people are slow to give critical feedback, because they are scared of offending someone. However, *feedback opens up a doorway to deeper learning and progressive improvement.* It is important to understand that the word 'critical' does not necessarily mean 'to be negative', as most of us assume or have become accustomed to think. Rather, to look at something critically can be to reflect on what went well alongside what didn't.

I am not sure what it is, but all too often there is something that prevents us from naturally giving feedback to those we are leading. Feedback is natural when we are in education, but it seems to stop the moment we finish our final assignment or exam.

I loved getting feedback in school, because it was the only way I really knew how I was doing. My teacher's feedback would help me see what aspects of a subject I understood, and it also shone a light onto the subject matter I found most challenging and needed to work on. This would allow me to focus my revision on the bits of understanding I lacked the most. The constant repetition of feedback and revision is what propelled me to get the best exam grades possible.

Like a teacher does for their pupils, a mentor can give leaders this same level of feedback in whatever sphere of influence they find themselves in – giving leaders an affirmation of their strengths and highlighting areas that will take their leadership to the next level.

For feedback and learning to be most effective, the feedback given by a mentor should not just be one way. It should be a conversation between the mentor and the mentee, as this allows for deep personal reflection and self-learning to take place. *The best reflection comes off the back of good questions*, so it is vital you get good at asking well-crafted and thought-provoking questions to aid the reflective process and to teach those you are leading how to reflect by themselves.

3. Accountability and safeguarding

I once went to a wedding where a well-known leader came to give the talk at the marriage ceremony. I was able to spend some time talking to this leader prior to the start of the wedding, where they found out that I was the youth worker at the church. The wedding was incredible and the well-known leader absolutely crushed their talk!

After the ceremony, everyone stayed around for canapés. While this was going on, I could see the well-known leader talking to a member of our church youth. Once the conversation had concluded, I saw the leader walk over to me. As they got to me, they asked if they could be accountable to me!

I was blown away by this statement. Why would someone of this calibre want to be accountable to me? I'm no one special! Nevertheless, the leader told me every element of the conversation that had taken place with the young person.

As I reflected on this scene, I was humbled and greatly challenged. Here was a well-known leader visiting somewhere they did not know, with people they had never met before. As a result, they wanted to be held to account for all their actions to keep themselves safe and to make sure the appropriate follow-up was given to the young person.

You may be wondering why this is such a big deal. Well, like with giving feedback, accountability is not always put in place as much as it should be. The benefits of accountability are that it makes people take responsibility for their actions, lessens conflicts, builds trust relationally and in areas of performance, and it measures progress/growth. These benefits, sadly, are all too often overlooked.

Mentoring provides a safe place for accountability because *accountability safeguards an individual from potential harm and halted growth.* Like with the well-known leader at the wedding, they kept themselves safe because they were accountable.

Of the young people I mentor, they are all accountable to me in different ways, as I am to my mentors. The accountability in these relationships covers various aspects of life, from faith and romantic relationships to internet usage, job responsibilities and leadership/influence. However, no matter what the area, the one thing at the heart of accountability is that the individual is safe and you are there to help them grow through loving them and abstaining from judgement.

There is a freedom that comes with accountability. If accountability is not a part of your mentor or mentee programme, I would highly recommend that you start it from your next meeting.

4. Frequent and consistent

While mentoring provides a great space for people to grow, there is one thing that mentoring must be, at every level, in order for it to be maximally effective. *Mentoring must be frequent and consistent.* As soon as frequency and consistency are lost, the value of mentoring is minimised and the possible leadership growth is significantly decreased.

If the gap between seeing your mentor or mentees is too big, then you will spend most of your time in each other's company catching up on the last few months. Catching up is important, but if it takes up too much time, you will leave the session together without having had space for the important stuff.

One thing I have started to do with those I mentor, to enable frequency and consistency, is to book in the next time I will see them before finishing a mentoring session. This may not be the best practice for everyone, but what I have found is that setting time aside in advance like this showcases how much you value those you mentor. This is very important, because a mentor must truly value their mentee, to allow them to have the best mentoring experience possible. *A mentee that is valued is a mentee that grows*, especially in their leadership and influence.

Summary: Everyone needs a mentor and everyone should be a mentor. This is how mentoring flows at its very best and produces an all-round growth in leadership for all those involved. When done properly, mentoring will provide a great space for people to be equipped in leadership, through training, feedback, reflection and accountability. So if you haven't got a mentor, get yourself one, and then find someone to mentor yourself!

23
Get Out of the Way!

Leadership is not just about getting the platform,
but being the platform.

During this section of the book, 'Helping Others to Lead', there have been constant themes of giving others opportunities and journeying with people to help them grow in leadership and influence. In all of this, one of the attributes a leader must have is humility.

We often think that humility means to think less of ourselves or to talk down our gifts and talents. That is not actually the case. *Those who walk in humility have assurance of self-security.* These people can accept and embrace themselves for who they are. They are comfortable in their own skin and are fully aware of their strengths and weaknesses.

When a leader can walk in this humility, it is easier for them to act as a platform for others, as they don't require the affirmation from the limelight and they are comfortable to work behind the scenes to champion others and watch them succeed. Stepping aside and getting out of the way can be difficult for leaders to do sometimes, but if we want to be an exceptional leader who maximises influence, it is paramount that we can get out of the way so others can thrive.

Author John Maxwell says that 'exceptional leaders do two things: they develop other leaders, and they work themselves out of a job'.[21] In other words, you have to be able to *release* others and *remove* yourself to lead with the greatest effect and build a long-lasting legacy.

As you have read through this book, you will have seen some of the communities and projects I have been able to participate in, some of which I was able be the pioneer of. It's amazing to be able to work as part of a team and to play your part in starting something new. However, like with much of life, everything has its time and you need to move on to the next season.

Although the time may come when you may feel like you are called to move on to something new, it is important that you do not forget about what you started or what you have been part of, because it's no good leaving something unless preparations have been made to make sure the community or project continues without your leadership.

In the process of releasing others into leadership, a leader should also keep in mind that one of the aims of leadership is to eventually make yourself redundant and do yourself out of a job. To be an effective leader, this does not mean that the only time you step off the *platform* or out of the *position* is when you are leaving, but rather that you

---

[21] John Maxwell, *The Self-Aware Leader* (New York: HarperCollins, 2021), p 50.

integrate and exercise stepping aside throughout your leadership, in order to equip others and grow new leaders.

Too often leaders can become precious about *their* platform – the place where they have their influence. So much so, they become unwilling to give others a place or an opportunity to lead. However, *growth will always be lacking in organisations when a leader becomes too precious about their platform.* No one will have space to grow and be equipped, unless you are willing to get out the way. Plus, you will never be able to do yourself out of a job if everything relies on you.

Whenever I have realised that God is calling me into something new and that a time of transition is ahead, I do all I can to make sure the transition out of my current leadership sphere is as smooth as possible. My aim here is to give as many opportunities to raise leaders as possible, so when I eventually do go, no one really notices I've gone, because I've already been getting out of the way of other leaders through my time in that particular sphere.

There are similarities between the two key points above, as both releasing others and removing yourself require you to get out of the way. However, I do believe that there is a tension at play here, when it comes to finding the right balance of leading yourself and stepping aside so others can lead.

You don't want to spend your whole time on the platform so that no one else can lead and develop their leadership. Equally, you don't want to spend all of your time out of the way, because no one will know you are the leader and therefore won't take you seriously in a rare moment when you are leading. Both scenarios result in a limited influence.

So how do you find the balance between being on the platform and being the platform, in order to lead yourself and release others? Well, there is no secret formula to work this out, especially because the practicalities will look different depending on the area of society you lead and have influence in. However, I would suggest that if you can answer 'Yes' to these three questions below, you won't be far off.

1. Are you giving people a good example to follow?

If no one's following you, you aren't leading. Furthermore, if you are to release others into leadership, it always helps if they have an example to follow. They need *you* to give them a real-life example of what a good leader should look like. Jesus Himself give us the greatest example of this, when He said to His disciples, 'I have set you an example that you should do as I have done' (John 13:15). As the disciples followed the example of Jesus, we must too, if we want to set the best example for others to follow.

2. Are you creating space for others to lead?

By being an example and giving others the space to lead, there is a strong mixture of exemplary leadership and releasing leadership. You have to create space for others to lead in order for their influence to grow. Remember, *good leaders don't just stand on platforms, they are platforms.* So whether it is you on the platform or you are being the platform, it's an all-round win for leadership and influence.

3. Are you working towards making yourself redundant?

This question is valid, regardless of the length of time you are expecting to stay in one sphere of influence. There will be times when you stay in one place for a long period of time; you won't always be moving on to the 'next thing' in life. For example, you may only ever have one job and then retire, or you may have many different ones as life goes on.

However long you stay in one place, one way or another your time there will draw to a close. So even if you plan on staying in a position for ten years, still have in mind that there need to be leaders who will carry on influencing in year eleven.

I had been leading the youth in the church for five years when I knew it was time for me to step aside and take up leadership elsewhere.[22] In those five years, I had been working as part of a great youth leadership team, with my dear friends Fiona, Jane, Jaime, Jess and Sarah. We had seen amazing things happen among the youth in the church and they had all significantly grown in leadership.

This was particularly seen through a once-a-month youth service we created, called Night Lyfe.[23] Night Lyfe

---

[22] I have recently started as head of Children and Youth at Ascension Church Balham.
[23] Christ Church Aughton.

was developed as a means to grow leaders. It was young people who were in the band that led the music. It was young people who did all the technology to make the service happen. And it was young people who gave inspiring and encouraging talks each month.

It was giving the young people the platform that made me realise that I had become redundant. They did not *need* me any more. They were thriving.

Although it was right for this season of my life to come to an end, and despite knowing that leaders should get to a point of making themselves redundant, fully stepping aside is not easy. When you love and value people for so long, they have a special place in your heart. As a result, coming out of that role was heart-wrenching for me, for the youth themselves and for the rest of the leadership who would be staying with the young people.

Going forward, there will be new people coming into the role I have left, and I trust they will build upon what has already been built, because what has been built is a platform for them to stand on.

Summary: The best leaders develop new leaders and do themselves out of a job in the process. For this to happen, leaders must be humble enough to step aside and let others grow in their own leadership. This can be challenging, but if a leader can manage the balance between being on the platform and being the platform, the leadership of the whole team will improve.

Conclusion
Never Finished[24]

*A true master of their craft understands that they
can never truly master their craft.*

I think it's fair to say that few people enjoyed the seasons
of lockdown, caused by COVID-19, in 2020 and 2021.
However, I also believe that those with a desire to learn
from any experience in life will have taken some lessons
away from those seasons. Personally, if I was to look at
myself at the end of lockdown and compare myself with
who I was at the beginning, I could clearly see how much
I had changed.

We will all see ourselves change as the years go by. Yes,
some of them will be natural, such as our body changing,
but there will be some deep internal transitions that take
place too. I reflect back every year to see how God has
changed me. Every year, I am amazed by the internal

---

[24] © David Gaskell, Andy Monks, 'Never Finished',
www.youtube.com/watch?v=JSVzJ2BcSCg (accessed 2nd August
2022). This video demonstrates the picture of going up a mountain, as
shown in this chapter.

transformation I have undergone. I always leave a year different from how I went into it.

No matter what season of life you find yourself in, change is always possible. There is always more that you can learn and new ways in which you can develop. Learning is like a mountain without a summit: you can always take steps to get higher and higher, but you will never reach the top, because learning is never finished – if you make the choice to keep growing!

This is especially true in leadership, as *a true master of their craft understands that they can never truly master their craft*. They understand that growth will always be possible. This is why every section of this book is important. There will always be opportunities to *learn in leadership*, to *take the lead* and to *help others lead*, which means there will always be opportunities to grow and get a little better in leadership.

I primarily wrote this book because I wanted you to see how young people can be leaders today. They don't have to wait until tomorrow, as the world suggests they do by labelling them as 'the next generation'. Rather, they can take their place in leadership *now* and have influence today. That is my story and it can be your story too!

If you are a young person, my prayer and hope is that you have read this book and seen how you can lead and have influence today. I pray that you have been able to look at yourself and identify the gifts and desires that you carry, and to see how these gifts can be used to positively influence others and the world around you. As you go forward, I pray you would be able to take any opportunities to lead that come your way.

If you are a leader of young people, I hope this book has helped you to grow in your own leadership. My prayer is that you will be a leader who sees young people as *the now generation*, that you will value them, believe in them and inspire them to have positive influence in whatever way they can. I pray you would be willing to give your time and energy to mentor, nurture and develop young people, while walking in humility so you can be a platform for them. Young people need good examples to be overseers for them (see 1 Timothy 3:1-13) and to guide them in the right way as they grow in leadership and in faith – which is why they need you.

There will be different parts of this book that will have resonated with you, depending on where you find yourself in your leadership journey. However, what I really want you to take away is that the journey will never be finished.

We need more leaders who are going to be a positive influence on the world and the people around us. I wholeheartedly believe this includes you! There is great value in your life, which is the very reason Jesus died for you. And because 'the Spirit of God, who raised Jesus from the dead, lives in you' (Romans 8:11, NLT), there is great value in you which you can pass on to others – don't ever doubt that truth!

Now is the time for you to take the lead, to help others lead and to never stop learning as you go. It's time to be a ship that takes people on a journey. To be an elevator that will provide a platform for others to stand on and go higher in their leadership. And to be a greenhouse that always has a heart to see others grow.

Now is the time for *the now generation*, to create the ultimate legacy of leadership and influence.